The Eightfold Path
and
The 8th Plane
of Heaven

JEANNE REJAUNIER

ISBN-13:
978-1539185604

ISBN-10:
1539185605

:

DEDICATION

This book is dedicated to the memory of a remarkable man, my great friend of many years, the late Roland Gammon, religion editor of LIFE magazine, President of the Universalist Unitarian Church in New York City and Dean of its All Faiths Chapel, author of *Truth Is One; The Story of the World's Great Living Religions; All Believers Are Brothers; Faith Is a Star; A God For Modern Man*; and *Nirvana Now* – and the person who helped Albert Schweitzer write his Testament.

As Roland said: "Because in my view, there is no separation in death, I feel that death is a part of life and that life continues as the divine adventure ... In reality, life and death are one, and are different aspects of harmony and happiness."

CONTENTS

ACKNOWLEDGMENTS

Thanks to http://creativecolor.org; to cover designer Brent Meske; and to our many eternal friends on the Other Side with whom we share this ongoing life's journey.

INTRODUCTION

The immense popularity of books on life after death, Heaven and the Afterlife has been duly noted in the previous five titles of the Planes of Heaven series. Rightfully so, a large readership longs to know what awaits us at the transition of death. Most books on the subject are based either on near death experiences (NDE), mediums' channeling guides and discarnates from the Other Side, automatic writing, past life regressions, brief Biblical passages, or information conveyed by subjects under hypnosis.

The unique material described in the Planes of Heaven books is of a different source, deriving from the personal experiences of a group of several dozen seekers who, over a period of decades, met Friday evenings in Pasadena, California, under the guidance of mentor, master teacher and Dead Sea Scrolls translator Mary Dies Weddell, whose extensive knowledge of ancient languages, esoteric truth and inspired teachings influenced thousands in America and abroad. While many elements mentioned in other titles on Heaven and the Afterlife are corroborated in the Planes material, our Pasadena group ventured into areas unexplored in other published works. Mary's message, "it's one world without end, amen," resonates today, offering the seeker ways of connecting to realms beyond the physical world, at the same time being able to gain invaluable practical and spiritual insights for life in the here and now.

Central to Mary's teaching was the science of nighttime soul travel to the spirit world, a practice mentioned in many sacred writings. Soul travel in sleep is contained in the inner knowledge of all faiths: Hindus, Tibetans, Persians, Egyptians, Greeks, Hebrews, Essenes, early and later esoteric Christians and others all avowed the reality of communication between the visible and invisible worlds. The science of nighttime soul travel is mentioned in the Bible and recorded in other sacred texts since the dawn of time.

The inner knowledge of all faiths stress that our physical existence on Earth and the invisible realms are interconnected, that life and death are one coexistent reality; death is not extinction – there is a hereafter where we live on in the manifold planes of heaven: as Jesus said, "For in my Father's house are many mansions." Located on every plane of the etheric world of Heaven are temples and halls of learning where, as our physical bodies sleep, we examine and evaluate our lives, enabling us as seekers to grow in wisdom and understanding.

The first five books in the Planes series have taken the reader from heaven's lowest planes through the Plateau between the 7th and 8th Planes. In this, the sixth book of the Planes series, we are now on the 8th Plane of Heaven. Here, Mary's teaching embraces her interpretive approach to the Eightfold Path, known to Buddhists as "the Noble Eightfold Path," taught by seers for thousands of years prior to the Buddha having rediscovered it, interlacing with our nighttime adventures in the heaven world.

And so, our group of several dozen spiritually interconnected minds focused on reaching the next rung in our ongoing search for enlightenment. In *The Eightfold Path and the 8th Plane of Heaven* we continue many themes begun in the first five volumes of the Planes series, but with new emphasis in new directions.

The 8th Plane is different from the other planes described in previous volumes of the Planes series. On the 8th Plane, we do the work of the Eightfold Path of spiritual development. This Eightfold Path isn't necessarily a religious path; it's embracing the spiritual essence of all life, bringing the inner life into manifestation in the outer, living life from the inside out. The 8th Plane has been known through the ages as the rugged path of the soul, though for many, there can be more pleasure than pain.

Most people associate the Eightfold Path with Gautama Buddha, who rediscovered this very ancient teaching taught by all the previous Buddhas. Buddhists refer to the "Noble Eightfold Path," the fourth of the Buddha's Four Noble Truths, incorporating the admonitions of right view, right intention, right action, right speech, right livelihood, right effort, right mindfulness, and right concentration.

Following the Eightfold Path, our attempt to change patterns of thought and behavior is accelerated as we undergo stepped up training in learning discipline to overcome self and circumstances. Our teacher Mary Weddell used the meaning of the Eightfold Path to express the balanced method of spiritual development through Color and sound, by "breaking old molds" facilitated through continuing nightly visits to the heavenly planes, through awareness, prayer, meditation and other spiritual tools.

In the Friday evening meetings where class members shared experiences from their night work on the Planes, review was always welcome. From time to time, we renewed basics so as to more firmly implant them in our consciousness. This was especially important when a new student entered the group.

Those unfamiliar with the Planes of Heaven teaching as presented in previous five Planes books may not immediately relate to some of the terms mentioned in this book: Color, the Planes, night work, the Sleep World, temples, tests, keynotes, keynote colors, the Channel and development are familiar to Mary Weddell's students. What do they mean to someone hearing them for the first time? If this is your initial taste of Mary's teaching, we present this brief orientation:

THE PLANES OF HEAVEN   The Planes of Heaven are expressions of the soul's growth and progression. We live in two worlds simultaneously, the visible and the invisible. Together, these two separate yet irreparably linked domains comprise the essence of "living in eternity now" or "living in immortality now." The Planes represent levels, dimensions, different states and conditions through which an individual soul passes along the way of spiritual ongoing. One comes from the Planes, one continues after death on the Planes, and while living a physical life on Earth, one may visit the Planes in sleep. Before we seekers can expect enhanced consciousness, we need to create chemical changes in the spiritual body, to partake of a new atomic essence that entering the higher life requires. We do this through training and self-examination in the temples and halls of learning of the Other Side, on the Planes of Heaven.

THE SLEEP WORLD   A place where the souls of those who are not in spiritual work frequent in their sleep.

COLOR   The Color path is a mystical journey toward soul development. From an advanced state of consciousness, our teacher Mary Weddell brought through from the Other Side more than one hundred fully tested color rays and their definitions that form the basis of her unique "Creative Color Analysis" course, which complemented our work on the Planes. These colors, shown as four psychological and five spiritual arcs of 12 color rays each, plus extended rays, are unlike any color system you may have been exposed to if you've studied other color teachings.

"THE CHANNEL" or "The Channel of our Being" - The highest spiritual colors, our birthright, are contained in the Channel, also called "the Keys to the Kingdom." This inner portion of a human being is the path of light leading one's consciousness to higher realms of understanding. The Channel is our spiritual connection between the earth plane and higher states of consciousness. While in the Channel, we bypass the lower astral realms and are never exposed to negative forces. We're protected. You can find a description, meaning of terms and rendering of the Channel at http://creativecolor.org.

Greater in depth explanations on Color can be found in previous books in the Planes series, particularly in the second volume, *Everything You Always Wanted to Know about Heaven But Didn't Know Where to Ask*, and also in the book *Creative Color*, by Mary and some of her students, or online at the above web address.

LIONS   We call the stumbling blocks on the path of development "lions on the path" or "lions along the way." The lion was the insignia of old Egypt and appears symbolically in all religions. We liken our undesirable faults to lions. They're in the lower consciousness. A large part of our work on the 8th Plane is to confront these lions and subdue them. We need to overcome these negative traits because they hinder our progress.

MAPS   Included in the second through fifth Planes of Heaven books are unique maps/charts of heavenly realms that cite more than one hundred locations in Heaven beginning with the lowest areas, leading up to the Plateau between the 7th and 8th Planes. These maps help us understand a more accurate picture of the planes. This current volume includes a map of the 8th Plane temples visited by our class. These maps of Heaven we share in the Planes series depict areas of consciousness beyond materiality. Think of them as illustrating vibratory rates and dimensions of reality in the invisible world where our spiritual bodies dwelled prior to our present physical incarnation, where we will once again inhabit in the hereafter, and which we can also access every night in sleep while we are living on Earth.

THE PLANES OF HEAVEN BOOKS For readers unfamiliar with the five previous books in the Planes series, their titles are: *Planes of the Heavenworld; Everything You Always Wanted to Know About Heaven But Didn't Know Where to Ask; The Kingdom of Heaven and 4th Dimensional Consciousness; The Afterlife in the Here and Now*, and *Living in Eternity Now*. These previous five books take the reader up to and through the 7th Plane of Heaven and the Plateau between the 7th and 8th Planes.

MARY WEDDELL Mary Dies Weddell (1886-1980), musician (piano, organ, voice), poet, seer, and philosopher, author of four published books, specialist in Egyptology, hieroglyphics, Sanskrit, Hebrew, Aramaic, and Greek, was a remarkable woman whose teachings I have followed for half a century on both sides of life. The underlying theme of all Mary's work is self knowledge leading to self mastery. Through two peerless original courses, "Creative Color Analysis" and "The Planes of Heaven," Mary enabled her students to see more deeply into ourselves and to understand more fully the awe inspiring structure and purpose of creation here and hereafter. From a very early age Mary was a natural clairvoyant and outstanding medium, gifts she wisely downplayed so that her students might develop their own powers.

MIRIAM WILLIS Mary's senior teacher who taught the Color classes.

Extended portraits of Mary and Miriam appear in earlier Planes of Heaven books, particularly in the first book, *Planes of the Heavenworld*.

****

CHAPTER I

When Buddha rediscovered the Eightfold Path, it was already a very ancient teaching, known to have existed as early as up to ten thousand years and more. Fragments of this ageless wisdom are found in Sumerian hieroglyphs and on tiles and stones from an era preceding the cataclysm that ended the Pleistocene period. The Eightfold Path is contained in the fundamental concepts of Brahmanism, the Vedas and the Upanishads; the Yoga systems of India spring from the same source. Its principles were taught in ancient Persia, Egypt, India, Tibet, China, Palestine, Syria, and Greece. The Essenes were devout followers of the Eightfold Path. The teaching appears in the Zend Avesta of Zoroaster, who translated it into a way of life that was followed for thousands of years. Scriptures describe an ancient path that was practiced by all previous Buddhas. Sometimes a six fold path is mentioned, sometimes there are ten yamas and ten niyamas. Guatama Buddha's sacred Bodhi tree is correlated with the Essene Tree of Life; in Tibet the teaching finds expression in the Tibetan Wheel of Life.

The Noble Eightfold Path is the fourth of the Four Noble Truths of the Buddha's teachings regarding suffering and its extinction, leading to liberation. The Four Noble Truths are: the Noble Truth of Suffering, the Noble Truth of the Origin of Suffering, the Noble Truth of the Extinction of Suffering, the Noble Truth of the Path that leads to the Extinction of Suffering.

Buddha's Noble Truths explain the reality that life is suffering, pain, anguish and affliction, its cause being grasping, clinging, desire or aversion, and ignorance of the three marks of existence: that all things are unsatisfactory, impermanent, and without essential self. On the Eightfold Path, one sees that everything in life is in a state of flux; that all that arises will cease; and that our very existence is based on impermanence. Existence is painful because of the illusion of our own identity, because of our ego focusing on itself as if it were separate.

Practicing the Eightfold Path offers a solution leading toward self awakening and liberation. The Eightfold Path teaching explains the Law, showing how man's deviations from it are the cause of his troubles, and gives us the method out of our dilemma. By altering distorted views and replacing them, suffering is eased; one develops insight into the true nature of reality and works toward eradicating negative dispositional traits such as greed, hatred, and delusion. Practicing the teaching is to reawaken within the heart an intuitive knowledge that can solve both personal problems and the problems of the world. This results in the conquest of the emotional nature and leads us to Nirvana, liberation.

The eight rays of the 8th Plane are: Ego, Healing, the Path, Devotion, Knowledge, Imagination, Discipleship and Love. These will be explored more in depth.

"In my teaching I believe the only solution to the mysteries of man's existence and of his toiling toward a goal he does not fully understand, is to seek the inner self. You cannot falter or fail in any way because you are beautiful, a living proof there is a God." -- Mary Weddell

*****

MAP OF THE 8TH PLANE

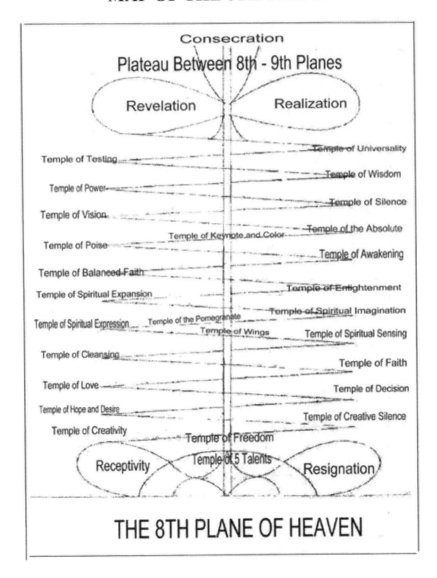

THE TEMPLE OF FREEDOM

As we embark on the Eightfold Path, we confront the Ego, first ray of the Path, where stress is laid on the mastery of pride and the control of likes and dislikes.

Having passed through the final tests on the Plateau between 7th and 8th Planes, we're taking a step forward on our upward climb toward truth and self knowledge. We've been through the Tower of the Soul on the 7th Plane, which continues upward through many higher planes. We recall that there appears an antenna of light that reaches straight up from the 7th Plane Tower of the Soul to the 8th Plane Temple of Freedom. We now find there are "steeps" from temple to temple, and that on every steep are stations where we stop to further examine ourselves prior to entering each new temple.

Approaching these Steeps of Heaven on the Eightfold Path, we experience a metamorphosis in rhythm and understanding as we pass through a great area of purple. One is reminded of the 8th color of the Spiritual Arc of Red as we enter into the beautiful rays of plum, red, purple and gold that envelop and deeply penetrate our being; we realize the meaning of these rays more than ever before: determination to follow the spiritual way, balanced enthusiasm, energy directed God-ward; carrying one's load willingly. The steady quest for growth of the 8th color of the Spiritual Arc of Red brings happiness and contentment.

There are seven words on each steep that represent seven days of the week during which we prepare for the ensuing temple. These stations on the steeps represent something beyond words, in that we are asked to get out of the mind, to go deeper and higher, and to listen in the silence for expanded meaning. We know we will never turn back, for we are the Path itself.

Fortified, we enter the Temple of Freedom, a massive edifice that stretches out into invisibility. Its walls are of soft pink peach stone carved in bas-relief adorned with many feminine figures in Grecian drapery. Some carry large urns, some carry scrolls, some lamps of wisdom, some musical instruments and some rare plants and flowers, including palm branches. Some of the figures are shepherds leading their sheep into vast areas that one can scarcely see, as they are lost in the distant mists of light.

The Temple of Freedom is erected on a foundation of faith, faith being certainty of things we cannot see. Without faith, we are as exiles in this life God gave us. If we accept the freedom of the Path, we realize as never before how important faith is.

Passing to the next degree of initiation, we're conscious of the unique power of choice freedom presents, and also conscious of assuming responsibility. We learn in this temple that we will be having testing requiring us to make decisions going forward on the lighted Eightfold Path, and that the first step on the path is to recognize the essential ego, the soul. The Figure Eight, representing infinity, is presented to us. Like the Möbius strip, a mathematical symbol, the inner becomes the outer and the outer becomes the inner.

Freedom is breathing in pure air, expanding in a heaven of unseen forces. There is no way but the way of light to come into the manifestation of the supreme underlying laws of God, in such a way that those laws may be enacted in our life pattern, used for the infiltration of God's power into our own and others' lives.

At every upward round of the spiritual ladder we're climbing, we need to be aware of being on each rung, understanding that we're safe, both feet, both hands on. The way is steeper, yet we are ready for it as we have trained for it. It isn't such a hard task if you do it one step at a time. Hunger within ceases as you begin to remember all the little things that blessed your life while they were with you.

This adventure is always open. Just turn and say, "For everything, thank God!"

*****

THE TEMPLE OF CREATIVE SILENCE

We land on the steep to the Temple of Creative Silence, called "forty days in the wilderness." Here we view our emotions, truth of self is revealed and we desire to do something about it. We use the 5th color of the Spiritual Arc of Red as we climb from the steep to the temple. From right to left, the 5th of spiritual red colors are: deep red, brown streak, and rose red. The deep red signifies awareness of the need to struggle with one's worldly self to overcome undesirable traits. It involves looking at that which one would rather keep hidden. As truth of self is examined, a deep cleansing takes place, which is often a painful process of going within to face habitual faults, together with the emotions and attitudes attached to them.

Key words to ponder in this temple are: creative force, great path, wordless prayer, meditative silence, patience, self mastery, and self respect.

MARY Creative Silence has a lot to do with our training in the Eightfold Path. You've accepted a challenge of silence in ways you never have before. There are other temples of Creative Silence on other planes as we make our way upward, but the temple here on the 8th Plane is the last one until we get to the 10th Plane. There is none on the 9th.

MIRIAM WILLIS The temple appears opalescent with a silver sheen. Resembling a cathedral, it's built of a soft pearl grey pearlescent substance, either marble or alabaster, very restful to the eyes. Beautiful planting is everywhere to be seen. The temple, from which steams a soft radiance, is located on an island surrounded by purest blue water. Two angels in garments of glistening mauve and white guard the temple's great door.

As we advance, we see the words: "Be still and know that I am God." There's a sense of being alone yet one with all life. Silence pervades our being, moving us to feel greater than we have ever been. A soft light emanating from everywhere deepens the joy we share with each other. In this activated stillness, we feel a kinship in understanding. We grow in consciousness in the short time we are in this temple.

The temple interior is the same in color as its exterior, except that across its surface waves of the entire spectrum of colors drift, expressing the latent creative forces of the Creator. The silence of infinitude broods. It is utterly peaceful, and we feel the pulse of a new creation within our souls.

Our Sponsor appears in a doorway over which is written: "I am the source and essence of all life." Following our Sponsor, we are aware of heavenly music and color abounding in glowing beauty and harmony. We are as the sounding board of the color and music that gently penetrate and empower our being in renewed creativity, as we move forward to become initiates of the Path.

When the music ceases, a profound stillness falls. Not a word is spoken, only the silence and solitude of the soul is questioned, with our response a wordless prayer. We then pass through invisible power that streams forth as we receive the communication of having fulfilled the vows of meditative silence. Invigorated, we pass through a spacious inner court canopied in the 4th color of the Spiritual Arc of Blue, casting over all a soft blue light. The color is a light cobalt blue. Gray overtones provide the holding force of usable power to control emotion and to prevent waste of vital resources.

We have formed a circle in rows of spiraled ascendance. The silence is broken by a voice declaring, "Creativity is the source of life. Your soul is endowed with the plan for your life. You alone can fulfill it." Our cup of joy is filled to overflowing.

We go to a small chapel within the temple where we share our experiences. One class member said, "To think that in the beginning there was God and the great silence. Tonight I have stood in that silence, and the silence was me, and I was a part of God. I will never ever forget this experience. When I woke the next morning, I was more conscious of my divine center of being than ever before. I felt it penetrate every cell, every faculty and organ of my being in increasing kinship with the divine and with all creation."

As one develops on the Path and extended vision is given, nature anoints one with the humblest as well as the grandest aspects of the Kingdom. We discern golden glints of truth within musty and antiquated myths. These shining facets free us from narrow and limited concepts, and every common bush becomes afire with God's love. God's radiance breathes and speaks within as your heart throbs to the spirit world. You realize what a glorious adventure life can be, but that it can also be a great trial, especially now that on this Eightfold Path you're going to look into yourselves so deeply. The faults you find in yourselves will come again and again and again, and you will recognize them as you never recognized them before.

MARY   The path is a paradox. It's a conditioned way that helps you to the unconditioned. Our true nature is always present; we're just not awake to its reality. Clinging to limitation and attempting to control phenomena obscures our true nature. The mind can lead us into many bypaths; appearances are deceiving. All sorts of things interfere with our progress; merely being of the world hinders us.

*****

THE TEMPLE OF CREATIVITY

MIRIAM WILLIS   Stillness in the Temple of Creative Silence fills us with peace and the energy of expectant faith. Through the endowment of this power we are able to pass through the seven tests on the steep toward the Temple of Creativity, where we're given seven words to ponder: Ego, God's love, power, self control, thought, divine imagination, and virtue.

This temple rises before us in spectacular beauty and in myriad tints and shades of color. I see it through a mist of light, like heat waves in a changing atmosphere. Presently, as we enter this light and become identified with it, vision clears and we ascend seven golden steps to a great door that opens of its own accord. We are in a magnificent court with many doors leading to other rooms. We are drawn, each to his own, across a floor of gold intricately formed in many triangles which seem to indicate a great purpose of power.

Creativity is the inner spiritual substance of love, the very life force that manifests in creation. Creativity is a gift to the soul of one who comes to this Earth as a developed person or one who has the possibility of development. Creativity is the inner spiritual substance of love, the very life force that manifests in creation, tempering the force to one's balanced receptivity.

I closed my eyes, soothed; a quiet, mysterious pleasure took possession of me, as if all the green miracle of growth around me were paradise itself, as if all the freshness, airiness and rapture I was feeling were God. Then as in a vision, little by little, everything around me, without changing shape, became like a dream. Earth and Heaven were one.

I was told by a teacher that language used in the Temple of Creativity was usually poetic rather than scientific. I was told to keep contact with the outer world of sense and its meanings, walk, talk, work and laugh with friends. The way to God lies through love of people; there is no other way. In this practice, nothing is outside of God. This is a secret discipline of life that constitutes the invisible leaven of the Kingdom of God.

MARY   In this Temple of Creativity, the power of the spirit of God opens to every sincere seeker. To each is revealed what his soul knows, why within him has been given the plan of his life. We see clearly that everything in creation is ensouled by a particle of God's intelligence, radiating in each and every one of God's creatures. We understand that intuition is the voice of the soul speaking when spiritual essence becomes divine guidance, and that only when we've reached Christ Consciousness shall we know the many roles man's soul has played throughout the ages.

Down the long winding stairs of gold to the altar in the center of the great auditorium's floor came hundreds of rejoicing angels, all holding golden instruments in their hands. The auditorium with its jeweled beauty gleamed with living glory. A silence more eloquent than words enfolded us all. We were as one being, as if all rivers of life had met in the boundless ocean of love. In the rose tinted twilight, I knew as never before the shining splendor of illumination and why our experience on earth was needed to know the revelation of the life of Christ.

The radiant faces of the angel choirs turned upward and the Voice spoke. Its words held the brimming cup of knowledge and faith to my seeking soul. Reverberating music became a soft refrain, as paeans of praise changed into rhythmic echoes. To me, the Temple of Creativity was a place to be always remembered.

JEANNE REJAUNIER   Each of us stood under an arch from

which poured forth a shower of streaming, shimmering ribbons of light energy the colors of divine imagination, inspiration, harmony, prophecy and a silver quickening the creative spirit. Inside the temple we walked in golden light past golden walls, hearing golden tones. The atmosphere is permeated with music, perfume and color activity. A fullness instantly swells in the heart. The entire experience in the temple is a joyful procession, as the expression of God's creative spirit is increasingly manifested to the soul. One is quite aware of a gushing pouring forth, of the outreach of love and the natural flow of things.

We entered a chapel with high ceilings and pews with high backs, where beams of light the colors of harmony and joy emanated from above. There is a great hall of silver lined with mirrors, bordered by a silvery lace-like effect like a picture frame. The atmosphere is shining and the large area resembles a ballroom. There was a cradle of the pink lavender color of aspiration wherein is nurtured the seeds of creativity, surrounded by a large item resembling a giant shawl of the 11th color of the Spiritual Arc of Blue, representing prayer sent forth to bring seeds to fruition. This color, sky blue, denotes spiritual life. Selfless prayers travel on this ray.

In this temple are rooms commemorating great creative periods where Earth has been receptive to the creative spirit. In the Greek room the nine muses are represented as caryatids. There is a Renaissance room. There is a large room filled with the 9th color of the Spiritual Arc of Red, a ray comprised of alternating stripes of light rose and light blue, the meaning of which is selflessness and consciously living in the Presence.

Where love shines forth and is poured into us, the inner light is ignited; we touch upon the great source of supply, breathe it in, and will now breathe it out to the earth in the form of expanded creative acts. Numerous things strike our fancy: large flowers, peach or pink in color, for instance. I also noted many examples of hitherto unseen art, new forms of artistic expressions which will be given to the world in the future. These are difficult to describe, but I was shown how they were executed.

Another interesting feature was the "harp of faith." Behind quivering particles of royal purple, the color of faith, was a golden harp playing music lovelier than any earth music, its tones ranging from deep plum to light lavender. I was aware that the symbol of the harp is an important one in the Eightfold Path.

In this temple are many fountains. Gentle soft light sprays of water shine and sparkle. All is rhythm of perfection. Myriads all together give off musical sounds in their play of water, blending with gorgeous color. As the fountains light up and their splashing joins into a symphony of heavenly keynotes, touching chords of joy within the heart, the soul identifies in a surge of inspiration and upliftment.

We may come close and learn of one fountain more deeply, or we can glimpse the whole and thereby gain a greater sense of pattern and overall design, seeing the larger scheme of things; or we may combine the two aspects, as the soul desires. The light here is intensely brilliant, and the flow of these bubbly fountains fills one with a greater desire to fulfill. The air we breathe is clear and health-giving; mountains, lakes forests, the sea, clear spring days-- none of these can compare with this clarity, with life-giving, soul-filling quality of the air here.

The fountains take on colors. Their activity creates a joy almost too great to describe. As the power fills one, the water of spirit is transferred to our being and our hearts overflow with happiness, with new purpose, strength, and awe of the Creator. We learn that to the soul with the backlog of development sufficient to enter this temple, creativity will burst forth – it cannot be contained where the desire is ardent to express the beauty of the flame within.

We were given the sensation of self expansion, becoming as if an enlargement of self looking down, as though we were the Father, fully in control of our lives, able to shape and express them with clarity and ease. Knowing ourselves as channels for the higher planes, our hearts overflowed with desire to give back all we had received.

ROWENA MEEKS It was interesting to me, listening to Jeanne, that I too saw a harp in my night work this week.

VIOLET STEVENS I was struck by the overlays of color in this temple. It didn't seem like mother of pearl, but as though there were transparent layers one upon another with flecks of all color showing through. It seemed of a material unknown on the earth plane. The general effect was iridescent, somewhat like that of the scales of certain varieties of fish or of Tiffany glass. A lovely place, not as large as some, yet a rare jewel of a shrine connected with a large temple. It is the Shrine of Soul Desire connected with the 8th Plane Temple of Creativity.

The interior has the same scales or flecks of color. This is a place where one gives soul longings free rein. Here one dreams large visions of accomplishment, and desires are reinforced by higher powers to have faith in their attainment.

MARY   We find so many chapels, places of worship and extra rooms in this great temple. Prayer chapels have been mentioned by many of you. In speaking of Violet's glimpse of the chapel, it's hard to find words to describe something that looked almost like the fish scales she reported--all the delicate shades you can imagine. And underneath, like in many a Tiffany glass, there's that layer of gold. Andrew, do you remember two weeks ago when you presented me with a great door with golden pillars? The door that Miriam brought is the door that you described.

MARGARET BRANCHFLOWER   I was given a brief glimpse of one of the windows in the chapel, a beautiful rose window. It had those pale, shimmery but very bright lights, mostly in pale, pale yellows, pale orchids and roses. There were no panes in the window, but the edges of the window, as if they were of stone, kept coming in and out and darting and changing as I watched. Even the receding of those little points had something to do with the whole idea, because they brought out the similarity of the words "recede" and "reseed." There were tall barrel vaulting arches overhead which seemed to expand and contract. This was bringing out the birth of an idea, a law, and a seed of life everlasting.

BARBARA STONE   I came back with several things very clearly remembered on several nights this week. At one time it was a tree that seemed like a strong oak, and as if I could see mountains. I woke in the middle of the night seeing a golden fleece-like object which I felt I recognized from what you said, Mary. Another night

I remembered some very beautiful rose bushes, and I was especially drawn to one that was a full blown rose that was very bright yellow in the center, that was peach on the outside. This seemed to contain a special blessing.

Then in meditation I received this: we went down to a lovely lake. A blue-green and mauve cast hovered over the water. Weeping willows drooped over the bank. Glowing white swans were so tame they came up to us and let us pet them.

My sister Jo was there. Most of you know that my sister made her transition to the Other Side not long ago. We were enjoying the beauty of one of the swans when Jo said, "Come on, let me show you what I've been doing." I followed her into what appeared to be a celestial conservatory of music. We went up rounding, gold glinted steps into a lovely little garden from where we entered a room that looked onto the garden. There were rich rose draperies at the windows. The colors kept appearing and disappearing, and seemed to come from the music we heard everywhere. A grand piano stood in the center of the room with filmy blue chiffon material draped over it.

A master teacher came in and instructed us in the art of composition. The master said, "Learn to write the music of the soul; then you will grow and expand in consciousness. Then others too will grow and expand in their development by the quality of your music."

I had the feeling that Jo was working with me on both sides of life in the music field, also that we're working toward musical harmony as expressed in the dispositions and actions in our lives, I here on the earth plane, my sister on the Other Side.

The master said to me, "Ask the wayfarers you meet on your earthly pilgrimage, why are you here? What is the main thing you want to accomplish with your life? This will help bring them to awareness of the lighted path and the need for their own development, and it will be a continual reminder of your own high purpose."

PATTI CHALGREN   I saw large expanses of color, like ten, fifteen, twenty feet of amethyst, a hundred feet of rose quartz.

These were all jewels – masses and masses of them.

MARY You were in the Chapel of the Jewels, dear, and the walls are those colors. Anything that you've seen in this world is there, only more beautiful. The Temple of Creation is for all mankind. It encompasses a great area. We went into many different branches and great wings of it. Everything imaginable is in the Temple of Creation. We felt that this temple is God's alone and we're invited guests. Everything is so delicately formed and so very beautiful. We carry away the essence of it in our bloodstream.

HELEN VON GEHR I saw two symbols. One was a beautiful rosette with petals branching out in different colors. I couldn't place it in anything.

MARY That's also in the Chapel of the Jewels. Others gave a window - Margaret and Patti. All right, you three people get together on this Chapel and see what you can do to expand it.

HELEN VON GEHR Tonight I saw a great harp. I didn't know whether the harp was a harp as such or whether I was the harp and something was going to play me.

MARY You are the harp that's playing.

MARGARET Rowena and Jeanne both brought the harp as well. As one of the eight rays of the Eightfold Path, the harp is a special symbol of the 8th Plane.

JOHN BRANCHFLOWER It's the 6th Ray of the Eightfold Path, Imagination. The definition: "One's nervous system becomes as a high strung harp on which the breath of spirit plays."

GENE HAFNER "At this point, one is ready to receive spiritual sight and hearing." The harp represents spiritual harmony, peace, and serenity.

MARY It's wonderful when two or more of you bring similar things. That's what we often do, match up our findings and see what we can do with it.

DAN Does the 8th Plane have a special color that dominates or represents it?

MIRIAM WILLIS The 8th Plane's key color is turquoise, the

9th color of the Spiritual Arc of Blue, meaning truth of self attained and realization of growth.

ESTHER BARNES   In meditation tonight, I saw a six-pointed star in that beautiful electric blue color first, and then, shortly after that, a lovely arched doorway. I thought it might be the doorway by which I entered. It was a soft gray sandstone, and had the most exquisite relief of Jesus on it, as if by a Leonardo or Michelangelo.

EVA TOTAH   We were speaking of a river. I was given the name the "River of Great Expanse." I was there with someone last night. We were riding along the bank. On one side was all land; on the other side was all water. The shoreline was quite straight, and I was right in the middle of it. Somebody was beside me. We were being propelled forward. It occurred to me that this couldn't be the sea or the ocean, because there was no ebb and flow of the tide; it was absolutely still. The water was placid, peaceful, and a great peace descended over me.

WILLARD STONE   I was with someone who made a beautiful object and gave it to me. There was this iridescent bowl with sparkly colored glass in it. It glowed. You could see through it. It had an unusually large candle in it.

MARY   There's your candle again, people, where you made your entrance into the 8th Plane.

ESTHER BARNES   Miriam said we went into a hall with a large circle. She mentioned there were triangles on the floor, and I remember seeing those triangles.

MARY   Miriam brought them back in gold, didn't she? Who else saw the gold? Barbara brought gold and Jeanne brought gold. Now see, we are really bringing back our night work, aren't we? When one right after another adds to our picture?

DAN   There's something else that came in, an important cup; it was so small I couldn't really tell the shape; but it was old. It had a pillar, as it were, and it seemed as if it might be the Grail itself. It was golden, and there was something inside that I could dimly see through the gold. One could hold onto the essence that was inside the cup just for a second.

MARY That's the Cup of Creativity.

BARBARA Mary, I wanted to ask about this conservatory of music I expressed.

MARY That's a room within the Temple of Creativity where you were with sister Jo, who has joined us in the night work. There are many of you who are with those you love at night, those who've gone to the other world.

SYLVIA HOWE Would there be a place where there are trees with crystals hanging from them? And a blue river and a dark sky and a mountain?

MARY Yes, you could see all that. That's where you were this week. The Temple of Creativity.

EMILY ROSEBROUGH I was in a forest thick with trees last night. The trees appeared to be oaks, but the lower branches were dying and falling off. There was a river running beside it. Although I didn't actually see the water, I sensed a river there. Was that anywhere near where we were last night?

MARY Yes, we were near that last night. I think you could bring back more if you try.

HANK We've been to other Temples of Creativity, haven't we?

MARY The Temple of Creativity starts on the 1st Plane and goes through many planes. We're often taken there to be reminded why we were created. In this temple we saw the miracle of what God bestowed upon us when he created us. We have quite a lot more self respect when we come away, more than we ever suspected.

FRANK CRANDALL Not long ago, Miriam gave us something about the eight points of the "Noble Eightfold Path," as referred to by Buddhists. They all begin with "right," and they concern what we're aspiring to do and become as we work on the Eightfold Path. Could we have those again for some who may have missed them?

MIRIAM WILLIS 1. Right view, or right understanding: an accurate vision of the nature of reality and the path of transformation.

2. Right intention, right thought, or right attitude: acting from love

and compassion. An informed heart and mind.

3. Right action: an ethical foundation for life based on the principle of non-exploitation of self and others. Right conduct in every area; behaving in sincerity, simplicity and grace. Thoughtful consideration of others always.

4. Right speech: to speak only in kindness and love, with words of encouragement and helpfulness. Clear, truthful, uplifting and non-harmful communication.

5. Right livelihood: earning a living based on correct action and the ethical principal of non-exploitation. Choose a right mode of earning that is honest.

6. Right effort: consciously directing our life energy to the transformative path of creative and healing action that fosters wholeness. Conscious evolution; moderate in all things; respect for self and all men. Fair minded in all transactions.

7. Right mindfulness: anticipating the needs of others; discrimination between our needs and our wants; to seek control of one's thoughts; developing awareness and mindfulness of oneself, one's feelings, thoughts, other people and reality.

8. Right concentration, or right meditation: entering reality through meditation; to plumb the depths and soar the heights; to find balance in life. Absorption or one-pointedness not just of the mind, but also of the whole being in various levels and modes of consciousness and awareness. Enlightenment.

JOHN BASINSKI And with enlightenment comes liberation, Nirvana.

MARY It surely seems easy when you're over there in the heaven world at night, where nothing deters you along the Path. When we hear these teachings on the other side, we believe it's possible to attain them. You come out thinking you can do that, because you've been in a vibration that has enlivened you to the thought that anything is possible with God. The heavenly paths are very beautiful if you once get the inner you to really achieve the concept of that Path.

*****

THE TEMPLE OF DECISION

MIRIAM WILLIS   This temple is for all people desiring spiritual development. The temple is located on the right side of your chart, your map of the 8th Plane. It covers a great space and resembles a large university. The grounds are beautiful, but one seems not so interested in the outer spaces. As we approach the temple we realize men of many races and creeds have read the inscription above the gates. It reads: "Each soul is potentially divine."

The goal of this temple is decision. Voluntarily and consciously man may choose between two paths, and his destiny depends upon the choice he makes. The soul embraces all that's recognized as individual and personal existence. The soul is asked to express its inner ideals and understanding in the world without. For this reason the soul is strongly linked with the mind as well as the emotional self.

How then can man attain his cosmic purpose? The answer is that long ago, he was given the great secret of secrets, which is to cultivate a love so great that it radiates joy and happiness to everyone he contacts, for then he is broadcasting living energy in Color.

The approach to the Temple of Decision has many buildings in a park of expansive lawns, cultivated shrubs and trees. The buildings are of a light, creamy fawn color with a very delicate pink tinge, and they are of sandstone. I recall pointing out a hospital to a group and realizing that many important decisions concerning surgery and sickness were made there. There were also buildings of science and philosophy for the same purpose, and buildings for resolving world decisions with groups of people quietly conferring. Others were walking about alone or sitting on benches under the trees, pondering and considering. The whole park was quiet and peaceful, the light soft and restful, all conducive to undisturbed thought.

The Temple of Decision is also of this light fawn colored pinky sandstone, very dignified Gothic architecture, like a beautiful cathedral.

One enters this temple alone. Although there were many people about, each person was alone with his own decision. In this condition I found two aspects, one passive, decisions of refraining from, and one active, the decisions of fulfilling one's recognized responsibility as revealed to the inner self in symbolic vision. Each person's vision was totally different from that of another, and the interpretation was given to the individual soul. One either accepted in solemn vows, thus pledging to continue on the Eightfold Path, or rejected the opportunity, postponing acceptance of such responsibility until later.

MARGARET I wondered if what I saw were part of this. First there was a pool which looked like a lotus, immensely bright, of a pale color on the yellowish side, and then there was the interior of a large church like structure, a corridor and a tower. I was at the bottom, which went up in diminishing pieces of innumerable stories. It was dark blue.

MARY It's a part of the Temple of Decision.

HELEN VON GEHR I had two visions. In the first one, there sprang up tall beautiful multi-colored tulips. Then I was facing a large sandstone building with a spire at the top. The spire formed a design; the basic pattern went into a cross.

I found myself inside an enormous room. There came a line of either priests or monks, each holding a candle. They went forward from where I was standing toward a long, wide stairway. They took positions one on each step, lining the stairway. The stairway went up a level, and on that upper level was a chair. Seated in that chair, in beautiful light, a master teacher was sitting. I couldn't quite hear what he said, except it sounded like "I am."

JEANNE I stepped into a high ceilinged forecourt with off white Doric columns. A large unidentifiable arched substance burst through a gossamer veil and became clearer and more manifest. This substance was comprised of the 12th color of the Arc of Spiritual Blue, the ephemeral-seeming light iridescent sky blue color of 4th dimensional consciousness, meaning the realization of man as a spiritual being in the oneness of the visible and invisible worlds. When touching this height one finds a blessing, a sense of comfort and companionship.

The substance was weightless, lighter than a cloud, with a particular charming quality all its own. Inside the temple was a large room that looked like the interior of Notre Dame Cathedral in Paris with the seats taken out. At one end was a large gilt or gold ornate frame. Small fluted swirling cream colored columns appeared every few feet.

Our group sat together in a large open space. In front of us on a platform were several ivory chairs carved in an intricate design, Chinese in influence. There was a crack or clap, and from both sides a group of about eight teachers filed in and took seats in the ivory chairs. We were told that what one thinks they're doing and what they actually may do can often be two different things. We're supposed to examine more closely, dissect, appraise and reach new conclusions. Where we haven't coordinated our ideals with actual earth expression, we have to face this and make the decision which way to go. It was said that one is often infatuated with an ideal and thus claims as his own that which may not yet be; do we really understand these concepts, do we really live by them? If not, do we want to in the future?

Following this, I saw an entire wall of the 6th color of the Spiritual Arc of Green, that beautifully clear blue-tinted emerald shade representing spiritual life brought to physical expression – so translucent and shining, a sign of rebirth. This color shows one who is reevaluating his life priorities and approach to differing ideas and problems. The blue overtone symbolizes higher spiritual reality merged into the physical energy of the emerald green. Blended, these two hues lift our consciousness as they're absorbed and applied in daily living.

In another area, I saw our group seated together around a huge table, about 200 feet in circumference. Another part of the temple reminded me of films and photos I've seen of the Moscow subway system. We were propelled through this part into a series of darkened roams where I saw Mary, Miriam, and several of our people, including Helen von Gehr, Ralph and Rowena. We spent considerable time in this place. Here, testing was divided into two parts. When I saw the others, part of the testing was over and we were waiting for the next half.

Outdoors there were many paths and walks, inclines and hills. It was easy to get lost there. Another night I was in an outdoor pavilion the color of light peach. This was a healing ceremony. Miriam, Violet, Sylvia, Eva, Katie, Clara and Bill were also there.

LOLA GRUBE   I remember in my night work this week an experience of being in a hospital. I got a message in the morning, "This hospital is all inclusive, serves so many." My husband was with me. We had been serving in an accident area, and I was very conscious of one person in particular whom we helped. I had received a message on peace. The message came first, and then the description of a chapel, the Chapel of Peace: "If you can recall the delicate beauty of the lovely tints of pale lavender orchid of peace, the blush pink orchids of serenity, the light blue orchid of brotherhood, the pink lavender of inspiration, and the rose of love in the stained glass walls which were arched and curved upward with an open top or ceiling, you will again know that there is a peace beyond all imagining, and from this chapel it emanates in an ever continuing stream inward, upward, and outward, blessing all. So you live in peace that others also may."

DAN   I have a question about Lola serving at night on the other side – could you say something about that?

MARY   You people do go out on emergency programs in your night work and help in time of flood and disaster when victims are coming over. This is part of the night training you're receiving. The people you encounter need earth help rather than spiritual help. These are people who wake and think they're still on Earth. They have to be convinced by an earth vibration they've made the change and are no longer in the physical.

VIOLET   I've been very aware this week of doing the work of the 8th Plane with the Eightfold Path, being given special training in this temple, where particular rooms are dedicated to definite purposes. In an area of the temple, one goes into darkness. The first room is of black marble. Here, one is shown all the dark things, which are often race inheritances. There's no light in this room except that of spirit. All your life is shown you up to the time you started on this Path. In successive rooms this process continues.

The second room is of dark greenish marble; here you're shown the traits of human nature; the third room is of mottled marble of a lighter shade. You see your indifference, when you failed to heed the needs of others, all the deeds of potential kindness left undone. The fourth room is of rose marble, where you see the passionate acts of your life; the fifth room is of a sort of orange brown shade, where you see the beginnings of the realization of the flame of spirit; the sixth room is yellow, where you see the kindly acts in service to others; and the seventh room is of pink marble, where you're shown the things of true spirit. The corridor's marble walls show your soul's reflection of itself and its development. After going through several corridors, we return to our group for another round of learning in another location.

Here, wide steps extend out from either side into the distance. Many other people are stepping upon the first step, as I am. Above me are gathered a group of the guides. As I stand there I'm asked questions. The same is being done for others all about me along the length of the steps. As we answer, we may then take the next step up, and so on. At each step, questions are asked that are part of tests to be passed before we may ascend seven steps. The questions stress fear. We're told that fear is one of the last lions to go. The atmosphere is like twilight, so I can't see clearly, but I feel and know that others are stepping upon the same steps as I am.

PATTI I had a brief flash of a hill that was covered not with foliage but with a kind of beige sand. At the top of this hill was a single building, a temple of solid bright rose red.

MARY Violet, that comes with the Cathedral of Jewels that you had. Patti has produced the cathedral where this corridor is. It's wonderful when two or three bring the same temple or the same corridor or the same chapel and can prove it to themselves. When you come out, the light gives you a shade of rosy pink, so that it would be the Christ Ray and the highest color you could attain.

After leaving the temple and being tested on desire for spiritual illumination, we were told only when man's spiritual perception is unfolded and he attains divine knowledge of self will he know God's existence within, and thus attain the consciousness of his own immortality. "Not by perfection but by grace shall I see my Master's face, not by the reach of mind alone, but by a heart that is his throne."

CLARA JACKSON I'm first aware of an orchard, and then walking between rows of white crosses which cleared away to a view of rolling hills. I next go down into a deep, darkened area and am welcomed into a tunnel entrance under a hill. I'm aware of some deep turquoise in a natural mosaic on the walls. There's an alcove or small room in the center of the tunnel where I sit and I put my toes into a cool pool in the center.

I feel more peaceful and sure as I start again into the dark passageway, now wearing a long, flowing robe. Soon the walls enlarge, becoming high and wider as they join a large bell-shaped room. I now have on a light blue gown, and this room is either flooded with a gold light or golden color.

Next I'm aware of going swiftly down a long white aisle with dark, smooth wooden benches on either side. At the end there are long rounded steps going up, a very deep rich rose. At the top I kneel on one knee and take something like a tray in my hands. I take from it and pass it on, and then another, and eat from both. Ahead is a beautiful concave worship or ritual center of a brilliant silver white with a large cross above of the same color. To the right I enter a low doorway of a rich medium rose into a little room like a study. This room is peaceful, quiet and comfortable, like being more at home than ever before.

Out the window I see that the room must be overlooking the edge of a cliff with pastel mists rising from below and many hanging plants live with new buds meeting in the mist from above. Everything has a silvery hue like the colors of dawn on a cloud. Again, as I perceive my surroundings, I wonder what will happen next, and I'm made aware that I now have this place within to meditate in peace and at-one-ment with myself at any time. I have another awareness of being outside near an opalescent shower, but it doesn't make me wet. As I leave I'm again aware of a structure shaped something like the arches of many wings in a circle with a round center with a silvery cobalt blue and white.

MARY That's the Chapel of the Wings that attaches itself to the hospital where these wonderful people go out to the work, at the very spots – the hospital that Miriam spoke of. It's a very good description Clara gave us.

VIRGINIA LOCKWOOD I don't know whether this was in the hospital or not. It has the coloring and the windows with the crossbars holding the panes of stained glass in the form of a cross, like a church window.

MARY Yes, a number of people have seen that. Didn't we say that people of all nations and creeds come. Therefore they would be in chapels very like the one some of you have described, and the cross would be very prominent. We identify there, and that's wonderful.

If you've been around that temple, you've met up with every type of a person, every nation, every race, and you realize that the aura is just as rich around each one, because each has found their inner divine self and are expressing it, and they express it very wisely. They're praising God within themselves. So many different types of people, all going to the various chapels, all taking the same tests we took. And that is very real—it belongs to the to the hospital side, Temple of Decision.

JEANNE Speaking of all the nations, I recall that two men spoke to me: one spoke in French and the other spoke in Italian over there.

VIRGINIA LOCKWOOD I recall being in a rotunda type building with huge windows in a circle. It reminded me of the circular rooms where the doctors go to observe an operation. I was the patient, and all these doctors were assembled in a row, looking at me, smiling with the kindest look on their faces. They had been consulting about my case, evidently, and they were joking and deciding what to do – decision again. They all had surgical gowns on; they had their little disposable caps over their heads, and they just stood and looked at me. They had been having a lot of fun when I walked in.

A young man in the back who didn't have a surgical cap on came forward. His hair was kind of light brown with a little red in it. He had round features, generous lips. He was the spokesman for the group. And in the clearest tones, pronouncing every word perfectly, he said, "We're waiting for our king to speak loud and clear."

MARY I believe you were waiting for the voice that speaks in every temple.

VIRGINIA LOCKWOOD I saw my mother. She was knocking on a heart shaped door. I saw her as definitely a seeker.

GRACE HALE Alma and I are kind of shocked because we didn't know there was such a thing as surgery on the other side. We wondered why people who've passed and no longer have a physical body would need surgery.

MARY Then you've forgotten your first planes, dear, the 1st and 2nd Planes we showed you the big hospitals and the reason for them. Discarnates will stay ill in their mind until they can change their thinking. And so they're prepared for operations, and they're cured; they come out of surgery and take their place in the heaven world.

So we have on both sides plenty of reason to believe that what we have done here on Earth has been very much a part of what they've done on the other side of life. I think many guided operations have been just that. If someone goes over and they're paralyzed, they've been lying in a coma, then they awaken on the Other Side, maybe a relative tries to orient them first; they make no impression, so one of the teachers dressed as a nurse starts attending them, and they respond to that uniform. It takes some time to convince them.

ANDREW HOWE Virginia said she seemed to be the patient.

MARY That's because she was the star in the play, was she not? It was hers. It was given to her. And it was revealed to her that her mother is a seeker too, knocking at the common door. The common door is the door of the heart.

Because we enter almost anyone's personality through the heart, do we not? You've seen a very old Dutch picture of Christ knocking at a gate-like door, a Dutch door, and they'd opened it just a crack. And he's standing, waiting for the door to open. Whoever conceived that has given us the picture that Virginia gave of her mother, someone seeking, not knowing just where you're going to go when you enter that door.

And you know, it isn't because we have fear, it's because we're so unused to new conditions, and we're more comfortable not to be disturbed, is it not true? To disturb ourselves and enter a new field of thought means absolutely taking hold of our intelligence to create a new mind in a new way, to be silent within ourselves and know that in this field, there's nothing to keep us from excellence. God does not deny his children bread. It's the bread of life we're seeking when we open the door, when we say "I will follow." It isn't what we do or what we assume to know that gets us into difficulties; it's the neglect of knowing one's self and not letting the soul guide and hold us at all times on the radiant way.

VIRGINIA ANDERSON   This happened to me this morning just before waking. I'm standing in an ornamental doorway that's like a very large picture frame. I'm very large too. I see myself oversize, filling the door space. My right side is close to the right side of the frame and I notice that my fingers are spread on my hip. My left arm is raised and touching the lintel of the door.

I'm seeing something quite unusual. Before me, suspended in space is a large thick slab of marble about six or eight inches thick. On its surface are beautiful patterns in mosaics of multiple colors. The atmosphere reflects and pulls upward all the colors of light and dark greens, light and dark blues, now soft medium and deep shades of red, now light and deep gold, then layers of light and deep blues and purples.

They float along in my view with purples changing to lavenders, then to pinks, and then they're no longer in sight. But coming into view above the marble slab is a small chubby *putto* walking in the air space. And that small angel form comes up and takes my hand off my hip and leads me out of the door frame. Together we proceed under the marble slab, and I experience a very safe, joyful and happy feeling as I move through the air space with my guide.

Again I'm aware of the mistiness of the flowing colors, but now they're not distinctly a series of colors; they're a merged blend with scintillating areas, as if sunbeams are piercing through them and expanding radiation in curves. My escort tells me something startling – I've been taken through a dimensional change from that large ungainly form that was waiting in the doorframe so that I could enter and become a part of the "nuosphere." I was asked if I liked my new state. I responded, "If this is Eternity, it fulfills all its promises."

I observed an extensive grove surrounded by giant alabaster pillars, and though I couldn't see the tops of them, I saw descending from them vines and trails of ivy. The panorama before me was that of a garden with flowers of many hues that were growing up out of sand. In the distance were lakes. There were groups of people sauntering, visiting, resting. Some were not in groups but remained singly. I was a singleton at that moment, and I accepted my new surroundings as if I were receiving an infilling of richness. I sought my companion to say just that, but he was no longer there. I had a very peculiar flash-thought at this point: there were no mountains here! Therefore, there are no abysses. Was this a metaphysical experience? Or a test?

MARY You experienced a great happiness, did you? You see, after you go through this corridor of mirrors, black marble, you come out and it's like a day of housecleaning. You come out absolutely cleansed; your emotions are cleared. And you feel bigger than you've ever been in your life, because you're emptied and you have the infilling. So I would say that was your spiritual experience in this temple.

PATTI Are there hospitals on every plane?

MARY It's according to whether people need to know. If I were to go to the Pattern World, and ask for help to find out whether I had a certain disease, I would be counseled. Doctors work on problems there and work through to the world.

Remember, our group is just one little company. We have every nationality coming up to the temples, but we all become one in the sight of God. We're one family. Therefore, whatever needs to be

39

given man to cleanse, to bring the greater infilling of spirit, he's healed. And if it's a hospital that he needs in his consciousness to receive the healing, he would go to the hospital.

CHAPTER 2

DAN   As a new person in the class, I recognize that Mary is taking me to the temples on the other side, and I've recalled portions of my night work, but I'd like to know more details about the mechanics of soul travel to the Other Side. Could someone fill me in?

MARGARET Nighttime soul travel is mentioned in the Bible and by all great religions, all of whom accepted as reality the communication between our two worlds. From time immemorial, spiritual teachers have taken students in their sleep to the heavenly realms for spiritual training; this is a part of the inner knowledge of all faiths.

ANDREW HOWE   Each and every human being goes somewhere when they sleep, whether to the Planes of Heaven or to the Sleep World. The Sleep World, which is mentioned in the Bible, is a rest area for souls who are not in spiritual work on the Planes.

MIRIAM WILLIS "Going out" and "being taken out" are two different activities. One of Mary's spiritual gifts is the ability to take us "out" to the other side at night.

MARGARET   Having mastered laws governing the ascent and descent of the soul between Heaven and Earth, Mary summons our spiritual bodies as we sleep. We're met by guides and teachers for night training in the heaven world, in the temples and halls of learning there.

DAN   Can you explain what happens to us during the "flight" or trip – this nightly adventure?

JOHN BRANCHFLOWER   Leaving the body through the chakra at the top of the head, the spiritual body forms, and in this body, the sleeper "goes out."

DAN How is this enabled?

FRANK   Our spiritual bodies are connected to our physical bodies by the silver cord.

MIRIAM WILLIS   This cord, which is attenuated when we're traveling out of the body, is referred to in Scriptures (Ecclesiastes 12:6-7): "Or ever the silver cord be loosed ... then ... the spirit shall return unto God who gave it," and was known to exist from time immemorial.

MARGARET   Our silver cord remains attached throughout nighttime experiences; it's severed only at death.

ESTHER BARNES   Starting at midnight, the class spends five hours in training on the other side.

LOLA   Every plane has temples and halls of learning where one's life is examined. You see your real self clearly through special mirrors.

ANDREW   Black mirrors reveal your detriments, clear mirrors your positive credits.

LOLA   We recognize memory patterns buried in the subconscious – guilt, fear, anger, criticism, resentment... you see the mistakes you've made and how you can change. We clear our negative emotions and patterns and we're given healing.

SYLVIA   We go through tests – fire, water and air tests. The higher the plane the more challenging the test.

ANDREW   The link between this life and the afterlife becomes stronger and stronger as you progress in the Planes. Visiting the other side at night in our sleep prepares us for the afterlife and enriches our present lives.

ESTHER BARNES   We're also able to reunite with loved ones who've preceded us to the afterlife. Eventually, when in death we ourselves cross over to the Other Side to inhabit that other dimension of reality, our consciousness will go with us to the extent that we've developed it on Earth.

ESTHER ESTABROOK   We're so blessed to have our Mary, but I've often wondered about someone who doesn't have an Earth teacher. Can that person go to the planes and work on themselves spiritually if they want to?

MIRIAM WILLIS   Anyone seeking development can visit the Planes. The spiritual body emits an azure blue light that attracts a heavenly teacher who will take that soul to the higher realms for learning.

EVELYN SWANSON   What can this person without an earth teacher expect?

MIRIAM WILLIS   At first, recollections may be imperceptible. One usually brings back only fragments to piece together gradually, bit by bit. But without a teacher one can still accomplish a great deal – clearing the past, balance, strengthening the ego, healing, growth, spiritual awareness.

DAN   Is there anything special we can do to enhance our night work?

MARY   First, we need to prepare for the night journey. There can be so many attractions, so many things to enliven our thoughts at bedtime. Or we're dead tired, so we drop off to sleep without preparation. Take a moment just before sleep to give this powerful bit of thought: what will my night training be? Before going to sleep, express your gratitude for the opportunity to go to the temples of learning while your body rests. Thank God; think of the safety in going into that Kingdom and dwelling there, to be taught how to live both there and here in the physical plane.

Then in the morning upon rising, express your gratitude for life, for sleep, for your nighttime experience, for renewal and a new day of possibilities. Record your thoughts and dreams while you're still fresh from sleep. The solutions to problems you may be having are often given through night instruction and be made clear to your conscious mind in the morning. This is answered prayer.

DAN   Are there special ways to help recall of our night work?

SYLVIA HOWE   Before we can expect enhanced consciousness, we need to create chemical changes in the spiritual body to partake of the new atomic essence that the higher life requires. It takes time and patience to effect a chemical change.

MARY   Patience is a quality we all need to summon if we're traveling that upper path and on the way to higher development. There's one thing I'd say when you go to these temples and you wish to bring something back: ask yourself, why would I not bring it back? Why wouldn't I know the way I've gone over so many times? Why couldn't I go back and forth and bring something to share? And then, in a spirit of true devotion, say, God, give me the light of understanding that I may carry back to the world something that will brighten another's pathway. That's being our brother's keeper.

We've used our mental body and our physical body, but our spiritual body has been unused to a great degree, not that we haven't been spiritually minded, but to what extent have we incorporated it as a body in which we live and move and have our being? That's where we're supposed to be equally with our physical body.

As we enter the heaven world's temples of remembrance, we're astonished to know we've forgotten so much we should have remembered, things we left undone because they were less attractive and appealing to us. The faults you find in yourself will come again and again and again, and you'll recognize them as you never recognized them before. It can be a glorious adventure and it can be a great trial, because you're going to look into yourselves so deeply.

When we go out to these temples, we're aided by the world over there; by God's love and by our waiting patiently, desiring the highest and best for ourselves and our loved ones and those we associate with. You've been incorporating within all the enlightenment and awareness you need in order to bring back the realization of what you're seeing and what you're being given in that spiritual mind. When the radiance of God speaks and breathes within you and the heart is throbbing to the concentrated effort of spirit, a permanent gift is yours to receive and yours to keep.

******

CHAPTER 3

THE TEMPLE OF HOPE AND DESIRE

MARY On the steep to the Temple of Hope and Desire, consider these words: "Hope is the desire for good, accompanied by anticipation; to trust confidently. Desire means to wish earnestly for; to long for."

As I climb a steep hill, I survey a temple that seems a mountain high, whose steeples touch the sunlit sky. The ethers are flooded with light. In the distance I behold fields of purple lupine. I questioned the heavenly teacher, "Please speak to me of this temple; it always seems so remote."

The teacher answered: "How may one grasp an idea unless the knowledge is already slumbering within the soul? As you explain this to another, you open a door in his mind, but the seed lies within the listener's heart before he responds. When the sleeper is aroused, soul is the teacher as well as the learner. Do you realize that through development you are your own teacher?"

I found many books in this temple. Books are records, symbols of man's mind, signposts along the way, yet there must be understanding within the reader's heart of the printed words' enlightenment. In times of need, a seer appears, one who has dipped his pen in the streams of creative energy, and the flame of his mind afire lures the soul to awareness.

I would ask you, dear ones, what are you hoping for that brings you upon this path, unless it be new wine to fill your chalice? Learning has been your quest; now your desire for knowledge brings you to the realization of life eternal. Be not troubled in your search, but hover your desires as a bird hovers over her eggs; know that alertness, flexibility, and open mindedness are the earmarks of unfoldment. Pass one day without irritation, for self control is a signpost, and sincerity must rule the heartbeats.

We all lose our patience now and then. Many people are inclined to believe that it does us good to blow off steam from time to time. One can be certain that in development, one pays a high price in losing one's temper and wounding another. He then realizes he has

45

lost self mastery, that his record of self control has once more torn down his wall of defenses. Now, medical science says that anger can cause blood clots. The coagulation of the red blood cells very quickly takes place in hot anger, and a thrombosis can be the result. But we also pay a heavy spiritual price.

MIRIAM WILLIS The 4th color of the Spiritual Arc of Red – red orange with a bright red midray – denotes anger and its derivatives. This color reveals a strong feeling arising from displeasure, antagonism, resentment, wrath, rage and fury. The color of grayed cobalt blue, the 4th color of the spiritual Arc of Blue, is very helpful to calm this emotion.

MARY The goal of spiritual mastership can't be reached by impatience, taking detours or skipping the hard places. It's never easy to hold onto our ideals. Something sinister is always seeking to take them away from us and make us cynics. But when we're strong enough to hold fast even in the midst of tragedy and disaster, we'll invariably find strength.

After being in the Temple of Hope, we descend to its twin temple, the Temple of Desire. We're told that in this temple we'll be given the key that unlocks the hope chest of reality wherein lies the answer to our soul's desire. Desire leads us forward to seek and opens the door to wisdom.

There are always hills to climb as the self is conquered, so be up with the dawn to climb, for the reward of the climber is desire fulfilled, broader and wider vision. Desire gave me the warm glow of love. Make its heart your shrine, for the day shall come when love will be the universal chant of life. God bless your way.

Through countless ages, man has wandered, ever seeking his way back to the soul's paradise. Only prejudice of the senses blurs our vision. Now as the Path stretches before us, we need wander no more. In the light of our immortal spirit, we may walk serenely henceforth. The rainbow of divine promise is ours. We know love as a dynamic substance that flows through the universe in living, vibrant streams of colors. For Color is to the soul what health is to the body, a healing power. Soul power is for eternity and will live when perishable things have passed away.

When a rosebud goes wrong, as some men say, it becomes a thorn instead. Yet God permits the thorns, and presses them into service, protective to the flower, like bodyguards watching over the safety of their beautiful queen. Desire for a better life grows in the soul by struggle and resisting evil. Courage is developed amid the temptations of life, that man may exhibit the true grandeur of his soul. He who climbs the Eightfold Path truly lives in the highest sentiment that man is capable of expressing. It is this sublime love that opens man's soul to clear guidance.

ESTHER BARNES I received wonderful spiritual energies in my night work this week. I was aware that Color, prayer, meditation, and singing were creating definite positive changes in me, and I was also aware of the Eightfold Path's definite tools. My understanding of the guidelines of the Four Noble Truths and the Eight Rays of the Eightfold Path were in focus. I recall a lecture on the Eightfold Path in one of the heavenly Halls of Learning.

MARGARET Our experiences in the temples of the Planes are so highly spiritual that we – at least I – wonder: is the Eightfold Path always this beautiful? In the temples of the 8th Plane it seems so, because we're fed extremely high dose energies for enlightenment and change. These energies color the trials and tests in our earth lives with new insights and new wisdom. Training in the heaven world enables greater understanding of what's taking place in our physical lives.

DAN The big questions throughout time have always been: who are we? Why are we here? Why were we born, what is the purpose of life? What is consciousness? How can we understand this life on a deeper level?

MICHAEL For thousands of years, the Hindus have told us that Atman– spirit, soul, the true self — is eternal, and that man's spiritual development occurs in many lifetimes, during which we pursue various directions on our way to becoming masters.

The Hindus say there are four possible aims to human life, known as the Purusharthas. These aims are: Kama (desire, love and pleasure); Artha (wealth, prosperity, and glory); Dharma (righteousness, morality, and virtue); Moksha (liberation from the cycle of reincarnation). Existence is conceived as the progression of the Atman, the soul, during many lifetimes, its ultimate motive being liberation.

IDA   We absorb color, energy, love, enlightenment and so much more in our sleep. Much of this is symbolic, with tremendous transformative energies bathing us. And we realize how important self knowledge is ..."be ye therefore perfect, as your father in heaven is perfect."

MIRIAM WILLIS Perfecting the self is a process during many lifetimes that ultimately results in the state of freedom from suffering and rebirth. This is the Eightfold Path.

MARY   We travel on our way to becoming a master. Nature evolves a man. Man, cooperating with nature, evolves a master. And we always need to remember, as the Buddha maintained, your resistance to what is, is what causes your suffering.

******

THE TEMPLE OF FAITH

On the steep to the Temple of Faith, we examined these words: "Faith, meaning trust, belief in the honesty and truth of another or of that which is unseen; and spiritual faith, the assent of the mind to divine revelation."

MIRIAM WILLIS   I heard a gentle musical sound like wind chimes as we approached the temple. I saw a string of colored lights like an arcade or corona above forming a gate entrance. A radiance of purple surface lay ahead, seemingly lighted both from within and without. Outside the temple, I noted exquisite tiny purple flowers and fields with rows of growing things, the living green of supply, given us through faith.

The temple is made of translucent glass or crystal, purple or dark amethyst in color, having both a cut glass effect in some places and a polished smooth surface in others. In some places one can almost see through it at points where the light shines strong, causing golden rays to emanate. The air seems sweeter and purer. Each glimpse of the Temple of Faith brings an increase of beauty and depth of appreciation and a wider breadth of understanding as the quality of faith brings to our lives. The soul embraces the temple with the scope it has attained.

MARY Upon arrival, we're led to a room where alone, we quietly await more light. Soon we're aware of being able to see with distinctness those objects which before were hazy and in shadows. As our interests are thoroughly awakened, darkness disappears and light comes to illumine the room. Now we can see all the conspicuous objects in the room. We're at ease in a large beautiful area with furnishings of rare and exquisite workmanship whose walls are hung with old master paintings. In the midst of our contemplation, the sun slowly rises, adding majestic and transcendent light to that already in the room. Slowly there comes to our consciousness the realization that a complete transformation has occurred in the colors which everywhere before were only distinctly apparent. All objects have taken on added hues and more delicate shadings, their beauty and richness many times intensified.

Under this flood of combined light, you find yourself saying with certainty that you're seeing things as they truly are. You know your limitations and that more vision cannot be given you at this time. As you bask in mute wonder and admiration, to your charmed senses the vision is complete. A voice speaks that brings added light to which your soul responds; your spiritual eyes have opened, and you are no longer alone; all about you are people of matchless beauty and loveliness. They reflect the heaven world, the delicate colorings of a world above and beyond all that we know as physical. Through this experience, all our mental faculties and powers are awake and active. We're asked to remember: the process of illumination comes to man by extending the limitations of his consciousness along the Channel of Color into the divine realm of reality.

LENORE The room we entered was hung with a purple crystal chandelier. The light shines through, sending shimmering rays over the room, which is of purple crystal or glass in a diamond shape. It has a gold tiled floor in a diamond pattern. In the center, a large gold and purple fountain splashes softly.

We visited several rooms and were filled with the atmosphere of many colors that lead to faith: the soft grayed old rose of the 12th color of the Spiritual Arc of Red, meaning seeing God in all creation; the 12th color of the Spiritual Arc of Blue, that color of light iridescent sky blue denoting 4th dimensional consciousness and man as a spiritual being who develops realization of the oneness of the visible and invisible worlds; all twelve colors of the Spiritual Arc of Purple, especially the 5th ray, the red plum of spiritual wisdom, and also the color of joy from the Psychological Arc of Red.

We recognize that there's no one totally lacking in faith, and how the snowballing effect of faith leads us on the path and impels us to heights undreamed of. We were shown our faith of today against that of the past. Thus we understood how faith the size of a grain of mustard is strong enough to take us long distances. We resolved to draw our purple cloaks about us even more frequently as we move farther along the path and grow in faith's healing, propelling strength.

MIRIAM ALBPLANALP In this temple there was a huge library with tables, shelves of dark brown wood, and high arched windows with crossings of inlaid diamond shapes. I was made very aware of being on the Eightfold Path, and especially of my need to aim for right view, right effort, and right action in my earth life.

MARY How do we stand on our lions? What have we done toward overcoming, we were asked by our teachers in the temples this week.

KATIE BASINSKI I wondered, could shyness be a lion? I felt somehow it could be.

MIRIAM WILLIS The definition of shyness as given by a noted neuropsychiatrist: "Shyness is a paralysis that comes from an exaggerated sense of our own importance." So shyness is one of the qualities one may need to examine on this Eightfold Path.

DAN Could you explain more about the lions?

MARY The lions are your bad habits, your set opinions, guilty pleasures and secret little sins, the jealousies you don't even recognize, the vanities you excuse or vaunt. Some lions hide from our awareness; some appear in unexpected ways. One might even consider some lions to be virtues, but they are actually traps in disguise. Many lions are subtle and hard to recognize, others we allow ourselves the latitude to indulge in, because we're sure we have no choice; we believe we have no alternative, lest we be unable to continue the lifestyle to which we're accustomed. Sometimes we're quite proud of our lions and wear them as a badge of honor.

HELEN MARSH   I'm sure worry is one of the most persistent lions many of us face and find difficult to obliterate. I know I do.

HELEN DE CANT   Anxiety is another lion in that category.

MARGARET   I've been compiling quite a list of these lions: anger, pride, greed, criticism, hatred, selfishness, laziness, dishonesty, envy, jealousy, fear, irritability, impatience, doubt, resentment, self pity, gossip, ingratitude, vanity, guilt, conceit, intolerance, dishonesty, possessiveness, prejudice, insincerity, hypocrisy ... the list is endless.

GENE   Another lion to deal with is cowardice.

MARGARET   The 3rd psychological color of yellow – medium yellow gray-green with a yellow ochre midray dirtied with gray-green – denotes cowardice.

MIRIAM WILLIS   Cowardice is a restriction, an unwillingness to participate for fear of physical or emotional injury. Antidotes include the colors of heroic courage, which is the bright red, 1st color of psychological red; moral courage, the 5th color of psychological blue – bright blue with a grayed cobalt blue midray; and the rich rose red, 6th color of psychological red, meaning creative life force, among others.

HELEN FLATWED   No one wants to admit to cowardice, do they? And yet we do face it in one form or another many times throughout our lives, so often without recognizing it.

MARY   Along the Eightfold Path, in dealing with the ego, stress is laid on the mastery of pride, the control of likes and dislikes. These lions, our undesirable dispositional traits, crop up again and again. These hidden things in us need to be recognized, cleared up and swept out. To change ourselves, we need to take charge of our mental attitudes and emotions. Self control over actions, mind over matter, mastery over thought, the purification of intellect, heart, spirit, innermost consciousness and the deeply concealed must all be exposed to the light. When facing the lions, you're cleaning house for both this life and the next.

We have vast spaces in this mind of ours, compartmentalized into boxes with set ideas enclosed in them that haven't been changed for a long time. The spiritual mind has been closed away as the attic to a house. So we do live in the basement many times, and then we come up to the first floor, the second floor. But there's that attic that's the last place to be cleaned, is it not? That's because you discard things there. So we have to take out what's in the boxes in these upper regions and not only air them, but also discard and change our minds in order to become enlightened people.

MIRIAM WILLIS   Suppressed negative patterns stagnate development. Negative emotions hinder progress. When we die, we leave with all our habits, flaws, and unresolved business. This is one of the reasons facing the lions and "breaking old molds" is important.

MARY   With the lions, our reactions are put through the microscope. Fear, pride, and anger can be transmuted into faith, love, wisdom, and peace. You can receive help for the negative dispositional traits you need to overcome as a part of the night work.

MIRIAM WILLIS   Working to achieve the next steep on the Path, we analyze failures that continually crop up, the little things we see in ourselves. As we recognize these lions, we temper the ego from lion to lamb.

MARY   People are afraid to break through the shell of their set ideas, but once we've touched the vastness beyond, we have a bulwark of strength to explore and discover the hidden; we're more ready to receive truth. As we grow, climbing the heights and plumbing the depths, we receive personal revelations needing clearance. Walking the path, you've known beautiful things, formed and formless, that come through inspiration and insights. But sometimes as we go farther, the beauty slips away and dark side is shown. We become annoyed. These annoyances break down the chemical forces. On the Eightfold Path, like a fine spider web, we keep spinning; after a while, the strands we've been spinning gradually change us.

ETHEL I had a particular experience in this temple regarding the lion of hatred in facing my likes and dislikes. I was very conscious of the 2nd color of psychological red, the combination of those ugly shades of orange and olive green heavily overlaid with stark maroon. The particular lion I have to face is one I had as a student – hatred for math. Maybe some might think "hatred" is too strong a word to use for an extreme dislike or aversion. But I think it's appropriate. I truly hated math. And when you spend energy in such negative, utter dislike, it poisons your entire system. You're living in discontent.

I truly hated math! Hatred, whether it's racial, personal, hating a discipline, a practice, hatred of whatever variety, is still hatred. It prevents positive action. It paralyzes. You're filled with this emotion to the extent that it interferes and actually prevents good qualities from emerging. This lion of hatred can be complex; it can lead to other lions, particularly to guilt and fear. I felt both of those, as expressed in my stubbornness and excuses. Since I did poorly in math classes, fear and guilt caused me to stay in a self-imposed shell, feeling inadequate, lacking confidence. It's really insidious.

I didn't hate people. I didn't hate any race or religion or political beliefs. But I hated, and hate is hate, no matter what disguise it comes in. I never realized how virulent this hatred was until I discovered it in my night work. It registers in the present because I never overcame it. It's too late to go back to school and try to enjoy math. Like most people, there's no use for algebra and geometry in my adult life. But I'm stuck with having hated those subjects, and it affected me, not only colored my developmental years, but I could have gone in more positive directions if I hadn't allowed hatred to get the better of me ... I need to erase it from my subconscious. I definitely need to eradicate all traces of this lion!

MIRIAM WILLIS We learn on the Eightfold Path that recognition is the first step in awareness. This is awakening. Next

53

comes intent, and a change in heart. On this path, we recognize it's possible to free oneself from the past by intention.

MICHAEL It's been said that the only miracle Buddhism accepts is a change of heart; otherwise we would never be liberated from the past.

JOHN BASINSKI Wouldn't the 2nd Ray of the Eightfold Path, Healing, be appropriate here? And of course, Buddha's "right thinking." Then we would need a color remedy.

MIRIAM WILLIS To remedy hatred, use the color of love, the 7th color of psychological red – pink rose lightly underlaid with pale orange. You could also use the color of philanthropy, the 8th color of psychological green, deep green with the touch of blue underlay; justice, the 6th color of psychological blue, which is composed on the right side of a bright leaf green and on the left side, light blue-green with a rose midray. Or you might also use the color of friendship, the 9th color of psychological red, which, right to left, is rose pink, orange coral, and flesh pink. Or use life's harmony, the 11th color of psychological blue, soft light blue with a touch of lavender.

*****

THE TEMPLE OF LOVE

MIRIAM WILLIS Renewed and sustained in the Temple of Faith, we enter a rhythm of spiritual balance, which enables us to climb the steep toward the Temple of Love. Here we're tested in fidelity to the immutable attributes of love on seven stations of this steep. Before we see the Temple of Love, we're lifted in gentle strength and enveloped in the exquisite fragrance of fruit and flowers. We're drawn toward the temple gardens, and in their midst, the magnificent, glowing temple itself.

The temple stands as a symbol of God's eternal love. As you approach it, you're aware of the force of God throughout your being, awed by the splendor of this temple, which is beautiful beyond words. Round in form, for love is without beginning and without end, its foundations are deep rose ruby, and it rises in majestic height until one can't see its infinity.

Three glowing mounds like gems of pearly opaline appear before the temple, surrounded with a sheen of transparent silk of gossamer satin. A pearly rose tinted glow emanates. Entering, we were surrounded by rose pink rays. Overhead was some kind of whiteness like a frosting on a cake.

To me, without any doubt, the Temple of Love is by far the most beautiful of all the temples of Heaven. Its entrance is one great slab of ruby stone. When you look into the depth of a ruby, you believe there's almost a heart there. As you look at the front of the temple, the roseate hues are so deep within the stone that you feel as if it were created in swirls. The temple's magnificence brings a glowing attraction to the Lord, drawing the seeker like a magnet in pure joy.

As one steps inside through the great portal, one is aware of light streaming through many windows that appear to be single gems of rich color casting soft rainbows everywhere. Growing accustomed to this, one sees many people in tiers. Every race and religious aspect that has expressed love is represented.

In the center of this area is a ruby altar placed on which are two objects of gold: on the right is a magnificent crown studded with precious gems representing the attainment of selfless love, man's offering to the most high; to the left is an equally beautiful chalice, the selfless love of man receiving into the vessel of his life divine supply which enables him to give selfless service. As we circle around, each one contributes the gems he discovers in his hand and they are added to the crown. The phenomenon to my mind is that there's room for all – no crowding, no confusion – and as one places his offering on the altar, he is at one with self and at one with God, enfolded in pure love for mankind and for all creation, with the realization that all that is, is love.

HELEN MARSH   We're shown that the true fulfilling of love is through the rhythmic balance of giving and receiving. It's as though we returned to this foundational love to beautify every other quality with the fragrance of grace. I drank in the rose bisque color of grace, which is the 11th color of the Spiritual Arc of Purple, feeling strength in gentleness and quiet unobtrusive love in the perfume of God's love. I understood that grace is giving in delicate, tender strength. It's retiring the ego that the power of spirit may manifest.

Reaching my ears were the pure delicate voices of a children's choir singing like a myriad of little angels. Entering the temple was like receiving an embrace, and walking each step one feels the divine caress of tender arms. The walls seem to be made of satin and the gleaming silver shone from wall niches.

An instrument I believe to be a higher development of the organ sent out powerful tones, the vibration of which was like a holy breath. This instrument has greater depth, tone, amplification, sonority and range than any earth organ, and its echoes have the power to reach the heart and vibrate within one's being even when the majestic tones are silent. As one expands in the presence of the power, one is filled with the sense of one's own divinity and that of all men.

In one room, diamonds hang from the ceiling as though strung together on jeweled chains. The light shines through them, making the whole room brilliant. All is light and one is filled with an abundance of spiritual power. A communion cup gives added capacity for love and forgiveness. We know we can forget past grievances. The color we see is the 10th of the Arc of Spiritual Yellow, deep rose to flesh, denoting the capacity for love in a person who has broken old molds and walks the way of love tempered by spirit, whose nature is intensified by the release of subconscious energy formerly used in maintaining those old modes of thinking. We know only love can make us whole; that love is the savior of the world; that Jesus came to manifest that love to men; and that the way is prepared by purity.

In another room filled with mauve, the 12th color of the Spiritual Arc of Red, soft grayed old rose, denotes universal concept of life. This, like others of the spiritual red rays, helps us to attain lasting changes in soul development. Appreciation envelopes us, a transcending that reaches out in wordless praise. One ponders the miracle of its uniqueness and is aware of kinship with others. It was here I was introduced to a new aspect of myself, at first a stranger, but then through the power of understanding and perfect love that casts out fear, it was accepted and incorporated into my being.

One comes here for enlightenment, inspiration and dedication, that the restlessness of uncertainty should become definite purpose. It's in such an atmosphere that visions are conceived and strength is given to carry them out. It's as though the currents of life were changed and thought patterns altered, steadiness gained and advances in wisdom realized.

There is born a certainty governed by sureness of intent that embodies past experiences and expands them into plan and purpose. One feels the overshadowing as though upheld by wings of angels, and there is incorporated knowledge of the power of love to lift and sustain. Burdens seem of no consequence; the soul becomes strengthened, able to pursue the course of action envisioned.

JOHN BRANCHFLOWER I had a sense of what Helen said, in being made more aware in my night work of right mindfulness in my physical life.

DOROTHY HARVEL I was shown an aerial view of this temple and saw the large dome and smaller ones as well as four minarets, courts, pools and tall trees. One is allowed to wander anywhere spirit leads them and sit on the many marble benches. Balance is gained and consciousness expanded into new territory. A teacher in the temple said. "We don't judge you; you judge yourself by the things you do." I can only say that those who visited here came away with wonder in their souls that such a privilege had been granted.

The great voice of our Master spoke, saying, "To all who seek for God and love, open the windows of your soul."

MARY The Temple of Love is set in the Area of Divine Imagination. That 4th color of the Spiritual Arc of Purple, the rose purple amethyst of divine imagination, is the open door to higher consciousness. It's a serene, rarified atmosphere of pure inspiration, the center of love and God intelligence. At the open door stands a statue of Christ reaching forth his hands to the world. Raising our eyes to the radiant temple created of ruby stone, its glowing love caused us to once again pledge our lives to God.

This was given as a parable by a master: When relative man, because of deep hunger for eternal values, turns his attention to the Temple of Love, he enters into an experience much like that of a bee. When the bee catches the scent in the lotus blossom floating upon the surface of a pond, he becomes excited and flies toward the blossom. But if he sees his own shadow in the water and becomes afraid, hypnotized by his shadow, he may fly round and round and finally through sheer exhaustion fall into the water and be drowned. Had the bee for one moment forgotten himself and rested on the blossom, he would have been safe.

Man likewise searching for God, his source of substance and values, senses the security of eternal satisfaction through the development of spiritual powers. He must have faith, never making a prisoner of what he requires. He must know the path of spirit is peace and harmony. This then would be practicing the presence, Christ's love in action.

Once the mysteries of love are unraveled and the solution of our problems reached by way of self control, we're charmed with love's responses and eloquence. Many times we're transformed when we realize a glimpse of boundless power through the creative force of love. And we have the wisdom to know no man is greater than his power to love. For love must be wise as well as tender. It must lift and guide the weak. As dearly as our precious Father loves us, he allows us to struggle for our development. And we have to remember, "Those whose spirits are stirred by the breath of the Holy Spirit, go forward even in sleep."

In Sanskrit literature I found an old meditation on the Temple of Love. "Let him find in his heart a broad ocean of nectar, within it a beautiful island of gems where the sands are bright golden and sprinkled with jewels. Fair trees line its shores with myriad of blooms, and within it are rare bushes, trees, creepers, and rushes which on all sides shed fragrance most sweet to the sense. Who would taste of the sweetness of divine completion should picture therein a most wonderful tree on whose far spreading branches grow fruit of all fancies. There the fruit and flowers know no death and no sorrows, while to them the bees hum and bright birdlings sing.

Now, under the shadow of that peaceful arbor, a temple of rubies most radiant is seen. And he who shall seek there will on an altar rare find the cup of life he is seeking awaiting him, and be aware at all times that love alone fulfills life's answer to man."

JEANNE   As I sat in this temple holding a candle, an angel was protecting it. It looked like the angels Miriam used to make. This was not a cherub, but a real angel. Then two others formed, and began to draw me toward the building. I asked, "Where are you taking me?" They said, "Where else, but to the Temple of Love?" And then I saw this beautiful ruby rose building and the coloring was a sort of soft pinkish glow, and then I asked, "Why the Temple of Love?" They said, "Because love is where all the answers are."

****

CHAPTER 4

THE TEMPLE OF THE ABSOLUTE

On the steep to Temple of Absolute, we ponder the following words in preparation for the temple: absolute, whole of reality, creative intelligence, doubt and self pity, pride, vision and truth. We also considered that in finding your own reality, wholeness is a sublime sense of something far more deeply interfused, and that the term "universe" reveals a great fundamental quality of creation in essential oneness.

We emerged through a series of colored tunnels, passing tests as we moved up the steep. The colors varied according to our individual needs. We relinquished trappings of self that inhibit our progress.

MIRIAM WILLIS   This is something Mary sends you on the Temple of the Absolute:

The philosophy of the Absolute doctrine is an idealistic one that conceives the whole of reality as one, limitless in power, which to us is spiritual in its nature. And as we know development, the Absolute is the Almighty God.

From Sanskrit I quote: "Behold the absolute, for it is love; my discipline is also love. I do not take the leather thong as whip, the pointed spear as goad, nor rule with iron rod of punishment. The faithful ones who follow me wield my love from deep within the human soul. I press my love into the heart until the sharp desire to serve in helpfulness is a goad to overcome all lethargy. I punish not with iron rod of fear, because the very loss of loving consciousness through unkind thought or act is punishment enough."

In the Temple of the Absolute, Four Absolutes are given as laws to live by: "Love is the great law;" "Thy faith has made thee whole;" "Ask and ye shall receive;" "As a man thinketh in his heart, so is he."

In other words, we apply creative intelligence to everyday living and thus attract the highest mental and spiritual power in the universe. The broader the understanding, the fewer rules required.

Dust the treasures of simplicity and thankfulness often, that their qualities may shine forth in your life.

From cloud to star there is a continual state of becoming. Dispel the enemies of doubt and self pity, for they are walls that screen vision. Living close to God will transform your life, but show it not in pride. Pride sleeps in the cave of knowledge, but humility opens the door to wisdom. Be not disturbed when vision is unclear, for there is a Christ embodied within the chrysalis of each human cocoon awaiting freedom from the womb of time. Vision is intuitive awakening; it is spiritual and deals with reality and the radiant Path.

LOLA   In the court of the Temple of the Absolute, we were entranced at the sight of beautiful shells of varied colors and shapes that were inlaid in a transparent, glasslike paving in a court where fountains played. One fountain gave an extra wide twirl and threw water over us as we passed. We came to a high vantage point and looked upon a compelling scene, a whole valley of twinkling lights.

Our attention focused on a large peace medallion which is over the temple gates. It's the dove of peace. It probably has gold surrounding it, and I believe the dove is of a precious material like alabaster with jeweled eyes. The inscription over the gate reads: "Enter the gates of pure faith, pure hope, and pure love, and worship him who is Absolute in perfect peace."

MARGARET   I saw apricot colors in peaks and angles that were darker to lighter to gold. Those who had passed the tests didn't need to tarry long, only long enough to reconnoiter and review what transpired on the steps toward universal love. This is the Temple of God—love for all mankind. In his infinite wisdom he has made it a temple without source, without definition, but whole, beautiful, complete for each person to the extent that each is complete within himself.

We review the visit. I walk along a golden aisle to a deep set doorway resembling a Roman arch. The frame is an extremely light peach, an extension of the Channel color of union of mind and spirit. The doorway itself is amber-apricot. There is profuse greenery on either side of the path as we approach the temple door. Now the door looks deep reddish purple, and it seems to recede farther and farther into the innermost depths of the temple.

We follow a passageway lined with divine imagination. Through the corner of my eye I see changing swaths of deep amber, purples, coral rose and a glass-like vase shaped vessel atop a crystal ball. At first it had two pouring lips or spouts, then three, then four. This is the heavenly symbol of the cellular division of life. You grew in that manner in your earth body; now you learn to give out God's love in like manner. When the process becomes so vast you know not through how many pores you are spreading this infinite love, then you are mature spiritually. Don't worry, you will understand love, its grandeur, its permeability, its splendor, its fragrance, its mutations and permutations.

BARBARA As I fell asleep last night, I saw many lovely faces. I awoke with a vision of a beautiful building of a rich blue, yet it seemed almost that it could have been a silhouette reflected in a giant lake. Then was something I had never seen before. It reminded me somewhat of Lola's medallion, but there seemed to be real beings impressed into the front of the building that were glowing in a sort of golden hue outside as if to invite us inside. They smiled in an especially welcoming and cordial way.

MARY That's a part of it. That's where the teachers stand. We always see them from a distance, and then when we go inside, we go with them to whatever corridor they wish us to take.

JEANNE On the way to the Temple of the Absolute, we emerged through a series of colored tunnels, having passed certain tests along the way, among them patience, endurance, and perseverance. I found myself beside a body of palest blue water beside a pale lettuce green hill, bare shouldered. The air was still and nearly quicksilver white in its intensity; I retained the knowledge of having emerged from darkness into a water test, having been cleared and passed. Cleansed from the waters, I emerged as the wind was blowing gently and split second later, I was completely dry. Next I was wrapped in an ectoplasmic box of my keynote colors, the lining of which was alice blue, the outer covering sky blue.

I was told this was my heritage, that thus fortified and clothed in my birthright, no one could take away or claim anything of me. I passed over a high bridge which seemed near a river or large body of water. A pathway led down to a sandy bend. Below, the beach was lined with colored crabs and crustaceans of turquoise and salmon, many of which had colored designs painted on their backs. There were also many exquisite shells and stones below. I descended and took another water test in this area.

Following this I approached the temple. All doors were wide open. The temple stood on a hill surrounded by foliage in a park-like setting with wide, long walks and a square or piazza in front. Outdoors was an open air library containing many volumes. One book with a rose cover, pale grey pages and blue type attracted my attention.

I viewed the temple from a lookout at the edge of a ravine, then approached it from a 90 degree angle. There were wide steps of off white color, either sandstone or limestone. The front doors were very wide; the side entrances on the wings were narrower. Entering at center, I viewed a square open hall which had grating high on the wall directly in front. This led to an auditorium. One or two reception tables stood in this area. The grating overhead was ornate and contained some lettering, the words of which I couldn't make out, but which Lola has told us. Inside the auditorium three groups sat opposite each other, and our group ended a ceremony by singing "Till we meet again," to another group that filed out.

I was introduced to a tall lean man in his 30's named Jack. I saw the colors of silver and opalescent around him. Around his head I saw what looked like lodestones. I was told we would be working closely together.

In a series of darkened rooms we were tested individually. My tests included meeting others on their level and not letting on if I am further along the path than they. It was a night of clearing, explanations from the teachers, sighting new directions, growth, progression, and new insights.

I sneaked a peek at Clara and Grace's rooms and found them both to be in good order. Then I was tested on honesty and firmness of purpose along with Esther Estabrook, whom I've been hoping to see in night work since September. Mary and Miriam were witnesses to this test. I also saw Eva, Violet, Lenore, Sylvia and Glenn. A lecture was about to take place in one of the rooms. Mary was going to speak, but the words had been illumined on a board ahead of time, so we looked at it. It was all in color. I had some other tests which I will bring another time.

VIOLET In the world to which we go at night we live in an atmosphere of love. Now love was intensified, for an aura of love extended out from this temple. One was conscious that the air we breathed was charged with it; it cast a sweet fragrance, a magic spell of soft, beautiful colors. A power we could not resist drew us into the temple.

We stepped through an open doorway into an atmosphere of interior charm, but now were added other gentle tones, giving forth the effect of an opal. It was as though love itself touched us. It entered into every part of our being: memory, mind, soul, and seemed to blend these, as the colors blended. We became attached, so to speak, to our true selves and to realize that this self is all love. Created within us was a tremendous desire to keep this close relationship and let the higher self have more control in our lives. Each one present was affected this way, for we had been given a bathing in love. We experienced deeper, fuller consecration until there was nothing left of the self but the purity of desire for utter cleansing.

We were baptized into a deeper relationship than ever before, which brought the oneness into being within pouring without. In this state, any thought or consciousness of the self as separate from its divine source would have been impossible, as would any separation from universal love. Then in some marvelous way we began to understand love. It was separated into its component elements, but we were not. We grasped the thousand ways love travels and the myriad forms of expression it takes, the everlasting power of its inexhaustible supply, and how love is ever sent forth. This love force overwhelmed us, overflowing from each to all – the people, the place, the universe, and we understood just a little more of God's love and that great love which is ever flowing from the risen and glorified Christ.

MIRIAM ALBPLANALP This, I think has significance in relationship to the last time we met. A week ago, while we were relaxing in the kitchen after class, it seemed to come from several conversations that while it was all very beautiful to hear these lovely descriptions, some of the men, having practical minds, appreciated the portions that had a more earthy dimension; it gave them a significance to what we were learning over there. I held that thought as a mental desire in the interval thereafter, and had two learning experiences.

This was from a glimpse of something that was symbolically on three levels. It was giving us something of how we're used as a bridge in our night training missions. The etheric realm finds it hard to always determine what the earth level of seeing and understanding is, just as the earth cannot get etheric reception except in cases of a specially developed human. Thus, communication is difficult for each, assuming they're seeing and understanding at a given level. For example, if it would be a war or accident zone, the earth soldier and the etheric helper would need, for a time, the help of a "pioneer interpreter" as to what each was seeing and acting, in order to focus each's level of reception to where they would more clearly glimpse the level of the other. Do you see? Very abstract. I believe this came from the Area of Abstract Understanding.

Another morning I just retained a glimpse of a blank TV screen with the outstretched hands, like the praying hands of Christ extended in supplication. This was a test in the interpretation of symbols – again from the Area of Abstract Understanding. After a while, I got the meaning at the spiritual level, which was that this is Christ Consciousness representing expanded spiritual vision and is symbolic of "Come unto me all that ye that travail and are heavy laden, and I will refresh you." It struck me as appropriate to right view and right action of the Eightfold Path.

MIRIAM WILLIS The Temple of the Absolute stands on a hill which is approached by a spiral path that winds upward to its magnificent entrance. This pathway is like unto that of the Mount of Renunciation, and as one climbs, the various clingings of self

65

that inhibit must be relinquished to enable one to proceed. There are many resting places along the path where one may renew his power of intent or remain. The color rays along this path way vary according to our needs of relinquishment.

The temple rises in blazing, exquisite light, and is of a substance like unto delicate rose pink quartz or crystals, breathtakingly beautiful, very high in structure. There are eight great entrances framed in pillars of eight sided delicate pink quartz. These lead to the inner courts of attributes of the Absolute fulfilling of the great law of love. The eight entrances also converge, making four, and the Absolute qualities are divided. After being subdivided they are gathered up again into the qualities of the Four Absolutes.

HELEN VON GEHR In a vision, I was in one of the forecourts where there was a fountain, the water from which formed a big arc. I knew this was water, but it seemed to be static and in little crystal balls all the way up. And within this was a figure, a beautiful spirit in white. Then the water disappeared or became as petals of a great white flower, and this lovely being ascended out of it. I saw a single rose on a long stem, and the word that came to my consciousness was "security." Then, for no reason that I could tell you, I heard "for whom the bell tolls."

MARY That's rather a promise, a symbol of peace. It's been given in England over and over again, this symbol of peace that comes.

HELEN VON GEHR Was Violet's this same temple?

MARY Yes. Hers went into the Love Corridor. I thought next week we would take these and divide them for you so that you'd know which corridor you were in, so that you can get a more complete picture, as much as we can bring in one evening. As we gather our wings, our chapels, our rooms, and put them together, after a while we'll have a temple. That's what we must do – get all of these where you have something that's positively a wing of a temple. Send it to us, and we'll assimilate it.

LOLA During the meditation and singing I had a vision. I had asked to go beyond the gate, and I wondered if we did go in. It seemed to me that I was on a very high hill. There was a tall tower we were going into, inside of which contained steps and spiraling. On all of these were white rows of figures, very beautiful beings. We seemed to be going up, and as we did, in the center there was rising this wonderful music with carillon bells.

MARY That's good; I'm glad you told me.

JEANNE Something I experienced might tie in with something Miriam Albplanalp said. I had a wonderful experience this week. I woke up in the middle of it, retained part of it but I was puzzled as to the meaning. I was told that if I went right back to sleep I could go to an "Area of Interpretation." I did so, woke up again an hour later, and received the interpretation. I thought this was miraculous. I wondered what the name of the place was and what plane it was.

MARY You would be on the 8th Plane, and as far as the interpreting was concerned, whatever temple you happen to have been in that night, you would go back to that temple and get your interpretation.

SYLVIA In the temple where those eight corridors go into four, would those corridors be Omniscience, Omnipresence, Love and Beauty?

MARY That's the Altar Room. In each corridor, even in the auditorium, love seems to be written in magnificent letters, carved in our minds as we come back.

ANDREW I received a description that the great door to this temple is heart shaped. There are many resting places along the way where we renew our intent. In the world to which we go at night we live in an atmosphere of love. Now it becomes intensified, for an aura of love extends out from this temple. We were conscious that the air we breathed was highly charged, and it cast a sweet fragrance about us in an atmosphere of soft beautiful colors.

SYLVIA The temple stands on high terrain surrounded by foliage in a setting with wide, long walkways. It was as though love itself touched us. It entered into every part of our being; memory, mind, soul, and seemed to blend all together. We realized that our deepest self is all love. We understood the thousand ways love travels, and the myriad forms of expression it takes to serve; the everlasting power of its inexhaustible supply, and how love is ever sent forth. This love force overwhelmed us, overflowing from each of us to all about us, and we understood love as exemplified in the life of Jesus.

MIRIAM WILLIS   In the Temple of the Absolute, we partake of such rarified qualities that as we continue our journey along the path of becoming, we feel an intense urge for cleansing. And there is also this urge and this feeling of need, a great uplift and encouragement. The soul seems to realize the great worth of its own divine substance and its inheritance; we also feel the urge to pursue the pathway toward fulfillment. And so for our meditation tonight I pray to be with you into the deeper realization of this wonderful process and opportunity that is ours to have and to share; that you would "know thyself," enter into the well of your being, rest there in the depths until the very urgency of your soul lifts you in the darkness. Here glimmers divine light that nothing ever extinguishes. This is your light, this is the essence of the divine spirit that dwells within. Breathe upon it and give it life. Let the urgency of your desire cause it to spring into a flame, and let that flame light the path unto your feet.

Blow upon the light divine and cast about the darkness of your being. Let it reveal what it will, and know still that you are the conqueror. Now face yourself, your strengths and weaknesses, attainments, and especially those things that cling and impede your journey. And now step down into the purifying pool and bathe yourself in the living waters, drink deep of the revitalizing power, and rise on the farther shore. Your old garments have fallen from you. You are renewed, enlightened; the old is left behind, burned in the purifying fires on the altar.

Let the fire of spirit purify the dross. Let nothing remain to cling to the renewed and cleansed self; enter with lightness of step; join the multitudes freed from the encumbrances of all that impedes and delays, and rejoice in the newness of your being. Toward this end, let us invigorate the colors in the Channel of our being.

HELEN DE CANT   Regarding the lions this week in the temple,

I was particularly aware of being given a greater understanding of greed, resentment, and gossip. Gossip, the 2nd color of psychological yellow – orange streaked with henna brown and dark gray green – was pronounced in my recollections. This color reveals a desire to talk idly about others, sometimes maliciously, behind their backs. I was given two colors to remedy gossip: the colors of friendship and life's harmony are both helpful in changing this trait. The color of friendship is the 9th of psychological red, which right to left is composed of rose pink, orange coral, and flesh pink; life's harmony, the 11th color of psychological blue, is soft light blue with a touch of lavender.

EVELYN   Jealousy is another lion that's hard to face, sometimes hard to recognize, that can be subtle and elusive. We don't want to acknowledge it. We ignore the signals; we deny the obvious.

MIRIAM WILLIS   The 2nd color of psychological green, orange heavily streaked with dark green, denotes jealousy. In the psychological realm of the aura, the intensity of the green energy and the orange color of desire display a fearful and suspicious nature, often vindictive. The rays of love, the 7th color of psychological red – pink rose lightly underlaid with pale orange – and generosity, the 11th color of psychological green – grey-green with lavender streaks – help overcome jealousy.

*****

THE TEMPLE OF CLEANSING

JEANNE   I find myself in a cool spot by a natural pool surrounded with lush foliage. There are bushes with delicate thin leaves as well as another bush with thick, velvety, heavy deep green leaves like those of magnolia trees. The air is filled with fragrances of oleander and orange blossoms. There is also a smaller pool with water so clear, pure, serene, and still, we can see our reflections. The refreshment and peace are so great we would like never to leave. Near this temple are many spots filled with beautiful waterfalls and restful corners with benches along the way.

In surrounding woods, coolness prevails. One's lungs are filled with a breath that is full of spiritual life energy. We walk to a circular place ten feet tall, 20 feet in circumference, made of white marble and surrounded with greenery. This stands in a small courtyard and is called the Fount of Ablution, meaning cleansing with water or other liquid, especially as a religious ritual of the hands and body.

The Fount of Ablution waters have a soothing, healing, comforting effect, with the ability blot out ugly scars and hurts and make whole. We are shown many scenes from our lives, things that need cleansing so we can proceed on the Path. After each painful picture or experience, there is the effect of an eraser, an action which blots pain from the subconscious like a whiteout technique in a film. Then there is a blank screen where the mistake or disappointment has been transformed. We find ourselves on a higher step.

Colored with the rays of harmony and tranquility, the air in a large corridor filled our lungs with life-giving energy. We were able to see the quivering vibrations of pulsating activity within the color rays and understand they were being incorporated into our lives as a part of the cleansing we were receiving. After this ritual was complete, in another part of the temple we were given a Grail Cup by a master teacher. Glowing white, gold and opaline rays surrounded the cup, and after partaking, we ourselves sent forth our own individual color rays of gratitude and thanksgiving.

MARGARET In the Temple of Cleansing, we face enhanced tests of fire, air and water. The visit to the Temple of Cleansing was a preparation for a lenten service. We entered a long glade featuring olive green with touches of silvery light. It seemed almost moonlight when we arrived at a corner of a building. To our left was a Greek like frontage with pillars, the whole resting on a foundation about ten feet high of small stones skillfully laid. The building was a soft olive green.

We go to the dark side at right and enter a doorway to the ground floor that went down two steps. Inside, the atmosphere is purplish color. Gradually there comes into view two touching pyramids, one inverted on top of the other. I'm given a personal lesson in balance and words of encouragement. Then my teacher and I go up a winding stair. When I momentarily recoil at the thought of more tests, my teacher enforces me with the words: "This is the time to press on and gain your advantage." I remove my heavy shoes that are filled with dread, and suddenly I'm wearing winged sandals filled with light. We emerge on an upper floor with a rotunda in the center. Large whirling circles of light appear, each seven or eight feet above the other. I can't see the top when I step inside the space. I see mountains or clouds with the rose color of love coming up behind them, and am given another lesson in color. I see a lake of fire.

MARY This is the end of the Corridor of the temple which Jeanne described.

MARGARET The lake of fire has russet golds, brilliant oranges and apricots reflecting a light I don't see. Excalibur, the magic sword of legend, appears in the lake and concentric circles spread out from it in the water. The sword handle becomes a series of birds and other visions which seem to be personal messages. I'm told to leave worn out things in the lake and I do so. The instructions are to cleanse them in the Lake of Fire, offering them to the absolution of the Absolute.

Next I see a cave or stage like a band shell of gray with a very pale spiritual color of the 9th of the Spiritual Arc of Blue, light turquoise blue, meaning truth of self attained. With this color, one sees clearly their fine qualities and talents as well as their negative traits. I realize that this shade is the major color of the 8th Plane. I also perceive the cave or stage like a band shell has the 10th color of the Spiritual Arc of Green inside and a brilliant rainbow above it. The 10th of Spiritual Green is sea foam green, the meaning of which is awareness of sowing and reaping, the law of compensation, "whatsoever a man sows, so will he reap," cause and effect, karma. This ray helps the seeker to be alert and receptive to the inflowing currents of soul wisdom to replace ego centered concepts. This is a balancing ray that encourages growth, that constantly challenges us to new goals and helps us recognize unrewarding patterns.

The band shell is reached over a bridge in the royal purple color of faith. I'm given several more lessons here. Next I'm told, "Awake. Go now to the kingdom of everlasting hope and renewal of faith. You have received your ablution and absolution." Then a veil of very pale rosy blue gray comes over the scene of my mind. We leave by the front door, which now has a tall flight of steps. I seem not to touch the steps as I descend, and I'm unable to look back at the building, though I try. Ahead I see fountains in front of a tall modern building that features sheer walls of black glass rising directly from the ground. It's the symbol of new things.

MARY That's the main corridor.

VIOLET A master teacher took me on a walk through strange terrain where I had never been before. The atmosphere was filled with forces of which I knew little. The air was clear to breathe, but difficult to see through. It felt like a mysterious yet not hostile wind that was blowing strongly was beneficent in some way which I was unable to fathom. I heard strange rustling sounds, awesome and lovely. My guide didn't speak and I asked no questions. We walked together for a long time, until the path became brighter, as beautiful pale lights of soft yet penetrating colors began to appear that seemed in a gentle way to streak across the sky overhead – not continuously, but intermittently. The rustling sounds increased.

We were climbing gently upward. At last I could discern the outlines of a formidable temple. The light about it was vibrant, as was the air, and I was filled with an intense power. I longed for the teacher to speak. When we reached the steps, he did so, urging: "Seeker, shed all that defiles." Continuing, he said: "One enters here stripped of all but the naked essence of intent. Only the pure in heart may enter, for your eyes shall not behold that which is unlawful to see unless you've been washed in the love of the lamb of God and so purified."

I became aware that others from the class were with me. Together, we entered the temple via the great doors into a mysterious and vast interior for deeper and deeper purification, deeper and fuller consecration, until there was nothing left but the purity of desire for utter cleansing. Again I heard the rustling sounds. And over that sound would come a more pronounced sweeping sound. This was repeated over and over again, until at last, I asked, "What is that?"

My guide replied, "The passage of the messengers of the Lord who speed to carry out his commands. It's their passage through space which you hear." Then a great Voice spoke and said, "Go in peace, my children, and a blessing go with you. You have received an added portion of the gifts of the Holy Spirit." Our group rose and left this temple.

JOHN BASINSKI Violet mentioned intent, which is an important part of the Eightfold Path. She also mentioned consecration, which is at the top of the Plateau between the 8th and 9th Planes.

DAN On the Eightfold Path, intent impels us toward a change of heart, resulting in liberation from the past.

PATTI I saw two buildings, one right after the other. The first was the olive drab, slate sides, no windows, just absolutely solid flat sides. I don't now how a person would get in it -- no doors, no windows. And then immediately the most gorgeous temple I ever saw, rectangular, seemed just like the most shining sterling silver, with spires all along the sides, very ornate, like the jewels of a crown. I don't know about the doors or windows, but when you get up on the hill where I was, you could see down over the roof into it and it was all crystal prismatic designs. I noticed there was one long corridor of the 12th color of the Spiritual Arc of Blue, light iridescent sky blue, meaning 4th dimensional consciousness and the realization of man as a spiritual being. Our understanding of the oneness of the visible and invisible worlds expanded.

MARY As you listen, you'll find how many people have brought forth the same harmonious colors, blue and rose smoke, pale rosy blue gray, turquoise blue, iridescent sky blue, and then after a little while, you'll conceive the picture of that temple. It will come naturally to you. Next time you go, you'll be very much impressed.

PATTI Was this crystal one a part of the temple or some other?

MARY That's part of the cleansing. When we're uncleansed, we can hurry past the waters of life. It took the hill of the Mount of Renunciation for Patti to look back at the glory of this temple. And there is renunciation in everything you give toward this Path, because we're in light and its activity. We do step aside from all the activities we're accustomed to. We've had a full week. Many of you saw where you had taken detours, and when you got back to the main highways of Temple of Cleansing, you were so happy to be back. You know you belong there.

VIRGINIA LOCKWOOD I wanted to say that the picture Margaret drew had meaning for me. I've drawn the same thing. I have the very same description at home in a notebook.

HELEN VON GEHR In a vision in class tonight, I saw a temple whose gates were of wrought iron design. Between this temple and me was a river that reflected perfectly the color of the sky. The river was going so swiftly, but there were flowers in it and I was able to pluck one. I'm sure the color was clear thinking and pure purpose, the 6th color of the Spiritual Arc of Red, rose red to coral pink, the first ray of wisdom, which brings the promise of spiritual sight and understanding of dreams and visions. I have a vivid picture of catching that flower before it ran away with the stream. Is that stream part of a temple?

MARY It is. That's what we call the Stream of the Temple. If we're carrying something that's passé, if it's not useful, then let's get rid of it, because if we have open minds, we're learning each day, and if the structural mind on which Spirit works does have open cells that must be filled with understanding light, then so must we houseclean, so must we be bathed in the Temple of Cleansing. God has blessed us with the opportunity for education and understanding. We've accepted, we've gone to that great temple and been bathed in understanding. We've walked where a beloved hand reaches out from the Other Side. You go across without fear, in faith. You've made progress.

MIRIAM ALBPLANALP I have something to share which would fall in that rather intangible area of explaining again, in with all the cleansing stuff. I was getting practice in two universal laws, the first being balanced energy, learning in a different way, like Margaret's symbol.

Monday I recalled water and fire tests. Wednesday it was water, fire and air tests. Symbolically, I was piloting a plane that was in difficulty. Something was tickling the back of my neck and I was having a struggle getting the plane down. By Friday, it was a cleansing test in air, then some kind of bird in a cage that was handicapped and unhappy. I was releasing the bird, so this combination of accepting responsibility and self control would then set free the higher Christ Consciousness represented by the white bird.

MARY That was given in the Temple of Cleansing.

LENORE I realized that water was cleansing the emotional, because in dreams my pattern was on water. Geometric designs were breaking up, and I figured that must be the breaking up of the emotional pattern.

MARY Very, very good.

JANE WRIGHT In this Temple of Cleansing, I was taken to one of the halls of remembrance and shown the very upsetting ending of one of my past lives. I was a young woman, perhaps 20 years old, maybe younger. I was wearing Puritan or Pilgrim clothing – a drab grey long sleeved, floor length homespun garment, together with the kind of white cap women wore centuries ago. I understood this scene as having taken place in the 1600's in pre-Colonial America. I heard a voice demanding harshly, "Give him the baby." Another voice accused, "Worthless! Worthless!" I was the person they were calling worthless.

I understood that I'd had a child out of wedlock, a boy. Either the baby's father or some other male relative wanted the baby, and I was resisting giving him up. They wanted this child because as a boy, he would be useful as he grew, to help with farming and other chores. For refusing to give over my baby, I was beaten mercilessly with a kind of wooden instrument, not a stick, not a club, but an object in between the two in size, and I was called worthless over and over. My body became saturated with blood from the beating. Then somebody picked me up and threw me in a forest. The last thing I experienced was being eaten alive piece by piece by a pack of wolves.

ESTHER BARNES This is such a harrowing recall. Was Jane given special help to ease through this horrible experience?

MARY In the Temple of Cleansing. Yes. We usually aren't shown past lives in our night work except in circumstances where it's necessary for a definite purpose. Jane's memory, while very difficult to relive, was given her because she was ready to accept it. It was important for her to realize how this trauma has affected her current life. Afterwards, she was given a very deep cleansing.

JANE I know the cleansing helped. Still, I realize I have a way to go in fully clearing the memory. The emotional realization that this happened to me is there in the background, behind everything. I shut my eyes and I feel tears behind them that start pouring down my cheeks, and the tears behind my eyes just won't stop.

ESTHER BARNES Could we posit that it's the 2nd color of psychological blue, ashen gray blue, the color of fear, that Jane needs to face and clear out in this experience? And what colors could she use to help do so?

MARY Fear is one of the deepest emotions to overcome. Its feeling is one of constriction and an inability to act freely. The 3rd color of psychological green, grayed yellow green, denoting shock through fear, is apparent in one who has suffered sudden fright or shock to the system. This type of fear creates a paralyzing effect in the entire body. The colors of basic understanding, the 10th color of psychological green, gray green with a blue-green midray, and heroic courage, the bright red 1st color of psychological red, both stimulate bravery and help in overcoming fear.

ESTHER BARNES Could we relate Jane's experience to the Eightfold Path, that the pain, the anguish Jane experienced is a major part of her underlying suffering in this life, that she needs to absorb the shock in order to overcome the extreme cruelty she experienced? We know in the Eightfold Path, the reality of suffering is a part of our existence.

GERTRUDE CLARK Jane experienced all that, and it's still a part of her psyche.

LINDA CLARK There's the law of karma to contend with, too.

MIRIAM ALBPLANALP To help Jane's problem, mightn't we think in terms of the First Ray of the Eightfold Path, that is, freeing the Ego through the inflowing power of God's love, followed by the Eightfold Path's Second Ray, the Ray of Healing, where the emotions are lifted so that the person is able to overcome their fear and attain peace?

MARGARET   And one also looks to the spiritual aspects of the 4th Ray of the Eightfold Path, Devotion, raising the focus of consciousness into the permanent physical atom, which in turn opens Cosmic Consciousness – as well as the 5th Ray, transcending the physical senses, opening to new understanding and expanding consciousness.

JOHN BASINSKI Right view, right understanding, right thought, right attitude, right effort – these are important in directing life energy to healing, and are part of the path of transformation.

MIRIAM WILLIS   We have a desire to go to this Temple of Cleansing over and over again until everything painful or corrupting is eradicated. And then we're standing clear, ready to go on.

******

CHAPTER 5

THE TEMPLE OF AWAKENING

MARY   Once a year during Lent, we go to the Temple of Awakening, where we're awakened further into the reality of the path into God's love. We experience morning, noon and evening there.

FRED   Awakening is an important part of the Eightfold Path.

JOHN BASINSKI   The realization of Nirvana is Awakening, waking up to the true nature of reality, to our Buddha nature, to Christ Consciousness, and to beyond the limitations of space and time.

DAN   The Noble Truth of the end of suffering is Nirvana.

FRANK   Awakening means a change of heart, awareness, mindfulness.

MICHAEL   It's possible to free oneself by intention, a change of heart, resulting in liberation from the past.

GLENN DIES   In the Temple of Awakening, we experience awakening very early in the morning after deep, refreshing sleep, to look out and see the receding stars pull down their curtains and retire to rest. We rise from couches of refreshment, stand erect, throw back our shoulders, and by the process of thought, let the winds of this sphere wash our faces clean and cause our thoughts to be reburnished. In the golden mist of God's love, with the impress of his face against the windows of our souls, morning on this plane is the children's hour. Now, as if led by imagination's hand, take mine, and we will witness the march of the children as in the early morning they act their praise to the source of all greatness.

See with me, then, a long white path leading into the forest. We look far on into the distance. We hear music, the voices of children singing in chorus. We see great regiments of them coming, hand in hand, along the path we are observing. The path has on either side many trees of astral plane life. Their branches overarch the path: weeping willow, stately poplar, maple, magnolia all reach toward this path, link. In the pale pink twilight, shadows deepen and throw silhouettes splashing along the path, creating golden pink radiance around the forms of the children. At a word of gentle command, the children stop marching. They are told to listen to the language of the trees, the language of the flowers, and the emotions of tender blades of grass.

On this plane the children can hear trees and grass in perfect harmony. A signal is given; the children walk on until they come to a clearance in the forest. They sit in a circle with their teacher in the midst; the children retrace their steps; they greet each creature they meet. Their laughter must have been caught from the strains of immortal music that floats from the most divine orchestra ears have ever listened to, for there is music in the laughter of children on this plane. There is beauty in the mellow light of this world. There is deep philosophy in the tender, noble life in this sphere, especially in the air of morning.

GENE   Next is noon. After partaking of a meal on this plane, we call to our side those friends whom we love. With true brothers and sisters, serene, happy, and free, we enter the Hall of Learning. We walk down a vast aisle. An instrument we call an organ, but for which they have another name, shakes the vast hall to its foundations with staccato shocks, followed by long drawn out sounds and vibrations that spell chaos. Through large tinted windows we see portraits reminiscent of Tintoretto. Outside, the landscape appears as the most gorgeous tropical regions of the earth plane.

Standing at ease, swaying backwards and forwards, we keep time to our own breathing and to the strains of music and the vibrations of the tinted light as it flows from the windows of this house of learning. At a given signal we stop breathing for a fraction of time to concentrate our attention on the speaker on the rostrum.

PATTI   Evening: In the depths of the ocean, the sea fish finds its home where deep currents sway ever onward. So we are, either actually or in imagination, deep down in the solemn stillness of the inner court of the Hall of Learning, and in the undercurrents of the ocean, one with the laws of nature. Breathing deep and thinking high, we keep perfect time with the speaker on the rostrum, for night has silently descended over this part of the spiritual plane, and the stars in the sky have pulled up again the curtains of their chambers, and a soft mellow light comes with quiet rest.

The speaker is talking on the great question of spiritual plane ethics, the study of the beautiful and the sublime and how they reveal themselves in the school of perfect equity and justice. The speaker's voice is musical; his personality is radiant with the things we hear in the environment and, deeper still, in the intense climax of our souls. So do all vibrations deepen to a white hot action and thought.

As the heavy jasper doors of this temple move back, white filmy tapestries are pulled down over the great windows; like glow worms of a forest whose thick phosphorescent beauty is caught from the love light of angels' eyes, pale pink twilight lowers until it becomes a strange, weird radiance that rocks our souls from side to side. Then as the period of evening arrives, all subsides quietly into silence as the stars dim to a pale yellow hue.

We seek the silken couches, gathering robes of purity, prayer, and inspiration about us. We hear far off the celestial choir singing the evening anthem. All on this Plane sink quietly into that profound sleep where even angels deign not to tread, as we go off into the dreamless sleep of this higher life.

MARY   We've spoken of morning, noon, and night on this spiritual plane. We've described the actualities of this sphere. We have pictured a descriptive oratorio of life in the three divisions of morning, noon and night. The symbol to observe is of a great star almost within arm's reach. Seek its polished surface to feel what the star is made of. Let this symbolized star eternally gleam before you, that your morning of life, your noon of activity, your evening into refreshing sleep shall be one whose thought, action and purpose will serve to illumine your soul. Then the voice of your life will sing, and in singing will reach to the master of masters, blend with his until all shall hear the divine song. I will be a silent listener in the house of the immensities of my God.

MIRIAM WILLIS Approaching this temple, one is aware of new growth beneath his feet, and must walk carefully among the tender plants. As dawn brings the light of sunrise, we see more clearly and realize how all things about us are awakening to new life in glorious beauty of sound, color and fragrance. Rare plants symbolically speak to us of aspirations newborn within our cleansed consciousness.

Awakening within is a buoyant possibility and reality. The journey up toward the steep of the temple has caused us to reflect upon the pattern of our lives and to deeply consider our place therein. We experience an urge to fulfill and a sense of responsibility for which we need much faith to bring things into clearer focus. Some seem almost blind as they approach the temple, so great is the light, so strong the requirement of faith that propels one forward. And now the temple itself appears as a great spiral, deep golden yellow to lighter tones. Its tremendous conical height is the palest yellow of illumination and mother of pearl of the Christ ray.

The entrance is so low one feels he must stoop to enter, but discovers he can do so standing erect, for he has become a small child. He discovers that others are of like stature, yet their faces are as mature as the age of the soul, and many eyes are filled with love and wisdom. One feels humble indeed and immediately resumes normal height. This made a deep impression on all who experienced it, and seemed also to open up centers of receptivity to enlightened response.

One became increasingly conscious of those about him as they moved in spiral circles around a great pillar of light that engendered an aliveness of keener awakening to each who was able to receive it. This penetrated the understanding, defining the qualities of responsibility, tolerance, justice, mercy, empathy, brotherhood and service. Then I heard these words: "Walk in faith and ye shall awake to reality."

VIOLET Far deep in the ground were subterranean passages that we each entered alone. The experiences were very personal. They were testings against fear, which is so often built up in one's imagination, or apprehensions of what might happen. There are fears that are the accumulation of race, the surviving cloak of primitive fearsomeness, but all seem real when one finds oneself up against them -- frightening noises and strange sounds, things brushing against one, hands trying to grasp.

Deep within, one has the consciousness that the only reality is truth, beauty and goodness, and that divine protection is always available. One moves forward, prays and asks for protection, which comes in a sweeping sweetness, a sensation of being loved and cared for that filled one with joy. As this state of consciousness increased, fear departed, for perfect love casts out fear. All of us successfully passed the tests. We emerged into light and found a beautiful curving stairway which we mounted for entrance into the Temple of Awakening.

No longer can one be submerged in fear, discouragement or gloom, for we've reached the place that is sunlight in the soul. The soul is sent forth in a higher vibration. In all tests, love is the answer. In this temple the soul truly grows. There dawns a beautiful sunrise whose flame enters the soul. Henceforth that flame of inner joy burns at a constant glory, reverence and worship, and is never extinguished.

MIRIAM WILLIS We spent most of our training hours in this temple. We were awakened and made aware of our responsibility to our world. We were told our gladness springs from the spirit of God. We were told of Christ's life, the great revelation of how the wealth of spirit was given one who had gained an understanding heart. All men must overcome to gain development. Do not resist the healing of guidance of the Path. Ask God each day for an understanding heart.

MARY We were tested on sharing, self control, self realization, vanities, growth, grace, and faith. The transition from one state of consciousness to a higher one is accomplished as we respond to clearer vision and are enabled to absorb deeper truths. The auric channel becomes wider and the path more familiar, bringing health, happiness, and a sense of peace and power. Bless you all.

EVA I was with Miriam and a group of young people at the seashore. It was a rugged sealine. There were caverns. The tide kept coming in, and as it receded, visible was red sand the color of love. Each time it surged in, there was more of this red sand, and it gave a very beautiful feeling.

MARGARET At the beginning part of the meditation in which I brought this back, I felt a wonderful feeling of love which had delicate colors to it. It was something greater than I had ever experienced. I felt it was the Comforter; it felt warm and light as the lightest eiderdown. Later, I wanted to know if I could see the temple's glade. I first saw the color of forest green, then lighter shades as well as large tree trunks with light showing between them.

I follow a path of light that goes to the left. It seems that a comet has been placed on the path. There's a large star at the head, and the path are ribbons of light that make a rainbow that carries me. I put forth no effort except to wish to proceed. The path almost stops now. I'm free to get off, but I choose to stay.

Next I saw what seemed to be the palest of pale blue lavender parachutes or balloons with baskets. Each one seemed to beget another one, and the cluster grew to quite a number. I asked if I could fly in one of those. They told me that the Path and the heights are the same. "You are in the first of these, sending out more and yet more parachutes on that high level when your feet are stayed on the Path. The Path is the heights."

There was a personal lesson expressed greatly in color. I wanted to know if there was a process of drawing earth to heaven and vice versa, and was told it's not necessary. "The star you saw can be your star on earth, the star leading the path. It is heaven laid at your feet with the colors of the rainbow to walk on. Draw energy from them. The Path is heaven on earth."

JEANNE Rounding a curve, I arrived at a solid complex of buildings shaped like a horseshoe. All was very still; nothing stirred. The buildings were of a sandstone color and substance, giving the overall feeling of a deserted city. Inside the same stone prevailed, and a blue atmosphere hung over several rooms. One room shown me was covered with a blue veiling under which outlines of furnishings were visible, and I understood I must lift the veil myself. I was shown how to find the potential in things that had seemed hopeless, how to revive and bring those things to life.

In an album I came across a series of old-fashioned cards in dark colors of amber and blue, puce and other delicate Victorian shades. The cards contained writing on their backs in a foreign language. I was aware of finding the God in all men, not simply those on the path where it is relatively easy to see, but those by the wayside as well. A way was shown me of a clearer and more accurate interpretation of earth events. At the end of the evening, the misty city I was in seemed to become royal purple, as if the atmosphere through faith had been cleared and I was now privileged to see what faith had accomplished.

Another night, I found myself in a grove under a tree, and heard the song of chirping birds. A temple stood close by. It was like the inside of a pearly shell, gleaming rose, blue, green and opalescent. I walked through a golden door of raining streamers to enter a large upstairs place with glass windows. Outside were trellises with interweaving crisscross designs of yellow, rose, violet and lavender. Below, the ground seemed like a schoolyard.

Alone in this room with a teacher, I was shown a further aspect of myself in need of clearing. Following this, at the end of a corridor I was shown a door of a shade of pink lavender, the color of inspiration. I wished to walk through the door and ask questions of the teacher, but was told I would have to find the answers myself in order to open the door. I immediately knew I ought to have known better than to expect answers to be given so easily. And then I had a small vision. It was disc shaped, gold, with twelve pillars encircling it, surrounded by an aura of rose.

BILL JACKSON I have a picture that I sketched of a building I saw Palm Sunday evening before going to sleep. It's a very simple, rather austere building with tall apertures.

MARY Where are your gates?

BILL I don't know. This is just what I saw from a distance. I was standing about half a mile away from it.

MARY That's the Temple of Awakening. Your gates are just in front of that. You would have to go in to look up and see that portion. You're in the first entrance, Bill. Come on in again this week and see everything progressed to an unbelievable level compared to what you remembered. Keep on sketching, and I think you'll probably bring it on through. You had to go through gates before you reached those many columns, and do you know the color?

BILL Just black and white.

MARY That's as much as you could see. Now if you'd gone closer and gotten into the greater vibrations, you'd find them turning mother of pearl, and from that maybe some blue or some pink, really defined on those columns. That's what we have, the interchange of those colors. Eventually, everything turns gold, and from gold into the apricot and rose pinks, soft rose pink. And before we know it we've said to ourselves, "Everything is gold!" We've just forgotten in the greatness of this emblazoned gold that comes before us, as if we had never been in such light before, nor had we ever conceived that such could be given us. That's what you've brought us, a portion of it.

JEANNE In the Temple of Awakening, the portion that I read first on mine, would that have been compared to your Evening?

MARY Very much.

PATTI This temple of learning we spoke of tonight, is that in the Temple of Awakening?

MARY We go nearly every night of our lives to heavenly Halls of Learning. That's where we receive the greatest instruction, because it's so simplified we can come back and bring it with us and work with it. We might not remember ever using it, but if we were to sit down and study it, we'd know we've used it, because some principle that hasn't been a part of our lives is suddenly created; we think, we act, and we haven't done that before.

MIRIAM ALBPLANALP I guess some of my vague thinking is crystalizing. I think perhaps it's attached to the Temple of Awakening, and it seems to be under the heading of "Law of Perpetual Balanced Energy," a more scientific way of the phrase "as above, so below." This has been pieced together following what I was saying two weeks ago. It started from the solid balanced triangles that someone -- I think either Miriam Willis or Margaret -- brought through. If you can visualize two balanced triangles meeting at a point, this would represent the solid energy structure; we did the three levels of bodies before.

Then if you took it in a figure eight swooping in this same form, that's liquid energy, comparable, I believe, to the emotional-mental. Visualized in an even finer form, you'd be making this same smooth outline of the figure eight that would be going into an infinitesimal point, going as high as the thrust, reversing and coming back so that in three dimensions you'd have this outer solid structure, the fluidic inner and the finer spiritual energy, all of which is concurrent and reversing back and forth within itself in an hour glass form. This then, is that multidimensional type occupying the same space-energy ratio that is related to some of the stuff our scientists are getting in, I think.

This degree of energy is related to the forces of desire and then back again to the forces of action. So translating this into our daily lives, what we intensely desire, and then we thrust that energy-desire upwards to get the guidance, come back and put into the action of carrying through; this then is our application of having the law of perpetual balance and a perpetual energy to carry out the balance.

MARY Thank you. Now, I would read that as that the first triangle would be the spiritual. There's three bodies of spirit, there's three bodies of the physical, so you've given me two triangles in perfect balance if they're linked within God's law. Then next, you brought me a figure eight, which is the path of light, and Christ came to the world and gave that Path. It is never ended, because it creates two worlds, two circles, two worlds without end, amen. So that's really very definite what you say, the power and glory of God himself. You have brought a scientific understanding of what we're trying to express. Thank you.

JOHN BASKINSKI To me, that also speaks of the Möbius strip and its relationship to the Eightfold Path.

ANDREW In the temples, have we been given talks on the importance of going beyond the limitation of time?

MARY Well, we're beyond the limitation of time when we're walking that path, because we have to think fourth dimensionally before we can even have faith in the Path of Christ.

ANDREW Is there any special thing we're focusing on? Is there anything I'm focusing on?

MARY You're focusing on the path, and that goes through about four temples we're going into. We went through the Temple of Cleansing, which was the first, and now Awakening, next we're going into Spiritual Expression, then Spiritual Sensing. And then we're going right back to what you said.

MIRIAM WILLIS And there are the steeps, too. You notice there's the merging of the three bodies. I thought of that when Miriam (Albplanalp) spoke.

VIRGINIA LOCKWOOD The palace of Versailles has a Hall of Mirrors. Do you think that it was possibly a reflection of a spiritual hall of mirrors?

MARY Oh yes! I could trace through the great temples straight all through Europe, especially, that has been given to some. I could trace the heavenly temples. I believe the windows are very like what their architects and artisans saw through visions. And I believe people have been so intensified in their work that they do climb on this ladder of seeing and through faith are given the work to do. And I believe the creation of many pictures have come through reaching into that invisible world and bringing out something that is not only different, but is an exalted thing.

And our poets absent themselves from their own thinking and go into this mode of reaching out as far as they can go, and come back with a thought. From that thought, they begin to weave and build, and we have a poem. When a man can hook up to that invisible power and express beauty in words, I believe he has been gifted. And God blesses one who can bring anything back from the Other Side, because they must have been given a gift.

GLENN I became conscious of myself and two other men being in the courtyard of what I thought was an old Chinese dwelling, which I later realized was a Chinese temple on the other side. Very shortly we were surrounded and taken prisoner by Chinese soldiers. It seems there was a war going on and they thought we were spies for their enemies. We were taken to a basement room and left under guard by one of the soldiers. Almost immediately a great light appeared in the sky to the north. Everyone became excited and started running in that direction. Our guard was distracted long enough for us to escape down the side hall which led to the bottom of an outside fire escape. We climbed this fire escape to the roof of the building and went to another side of the building where there were no people around.

The other two men, like the people below, wanted to go see what was causing a great light in the sky. Personally, I wasn't curious, as I seemed to know what the light was all about. I did not try to explain the light to these other two men, nor did I try to stop them from going to find out. At the edge of the roof, we discovered the building was three stories high; the distance to the ground was approximately thirty-five feet.

One man jumped immediately, picked himself up and started running with a distinct limp, toward the light. The other man jumped soon after that but didn't get up right away. He finally got up after a few minutes and hobbled off toward the light in the sky. In the meantime I knew I had to get away from the building and the soldiers, and was wanting to jump, but was considering what effect it would have on my crippled knee. I was able to convince myself that if I really had the faith that I professed to have in God, there was no danger of getting hurt, so I jumped. To my utter surprise I only dropped about four or five feet, and lit on the framework of some large steel girders which mysteriously appeared out of nowhere, and I knew then that my faith in God had been fulfilled.

MARY That's a test of fear and faith.

LOU I had a wonderful experience in just what we've been talking about. I think all my life I've been afraid of having to take responsibility. There's a fear, you know, of not being able to come through as we'd like. That lion of fear, again! So this past week has been an awakening for me in what the path can do for you, all our training, and how devotedly these dear ones on the other side come through when they're called on to help in an endeavor.

I had an experience one morning, a symbol given me that I was receiving protection. It was a dream of many hats, none of them decorated. It seemed so strange to me, so I asked for an explanation. It was that this was a symbol being given me for protection. There was such joy in the activities of the past weeks, everything came through and it's a wonderful proof of how life can be lived.

PATTI   Mary, we often speak of fear as being one of the biggest lions. Could you suggest the source of oversensitivity which makes you too easily hurt, so you retire within yourself? Is this also fear?

MARY   It's of the family of fear. It may also be a false pride.

ESTHER ESTABROOK   Could you say something about false pride and the colors involved?

MARY   We have the 11th color of psychological red, soft red orange streaked with purple, meaning pride. This is a balanced ray of rightful pride, absent of conceit. Pride can be the result of successfully using faith to fulfill a desire. Self esteem and self respect are aspects of pride. Seen aurically, the orange has a thin veiling of purple. If the colors are fused, a brown purple results, indicating false pride and its unpleasant relatives – conceit, disdain, haughtiness and arrogance.

PATTI   When you want to forgive and be forgiven, is there a special best color for forgiveness?

MARY   Yes. First of all you'll have to have a faith, won't you? And from that royal purple color of faith, I should go into all the lavender shades, the softest shades of lavender and rose, and I would end with a fuchsia centered gate. You've gone half the way when you desire forgiveness.

ANDREW   All these beautiful, positive energies and colors ... they're part of awakening, they're integral to the Eightfold Path ... awakening is key to overcoming.

JOHN   Intent and awakening are closely related on the Path. Awakening involves identifying and acknowledging our lions and being cleared of them. They're false, they're impediments. We need to conquer them.

ANDREW We're following this Eightfold Path that has come down through the ages, which was known for thousands of years before Buddha rediscovered it. In Palestine and Syria the brotherhood, known as the Essene Brotherhood, and in Egypt, the Therapeutae or healers, taught it. Jesus, who was a member of the Essenes, taught it. In the 19th century, British historian Godfrey Higgins sought to uncover the most ancient, universal religion from which all later creeds and doctrines sprang which once covered the entire world. The more we probe, the more we see the similarity of the Eightfold Path and how it comes from remote antiquity.

JOHN BASINSKI Divine wisdom tells us that the universe is the expression of a supreme conscious life, whether we call it God, Yahweh, the Absolute, Universal Mind, Jehovah, the Elohim, or countless other names. Every man has God within, a direct celestial ray from the One True Source.

RALPH I saw a big flat dish the other day, about five feet across with a bottle blue. At the center of it was a very small candlelight that made the whole dish fluoresce.

MARY The ocean of understanding is being lit. Well, carry your light! That's what you're supposed to do!

ANDREW I didn't know they had night and day on the Planes.

MARY We had that experience as an awakening to life there. We're given the experience so that in going over, we have some concept that we're going to live over there just as we do here. We're going to awaken in the morning. We're going to share at noon. At night we're going to rest in God's love. And that is world without end, a phrase you'll keep in your consciousness. You'll find it winding in and out of all of this teaching, we believe that in opening the door into that world, we're going to relive. We'll find that we'll be doing many things alone after we get over there. So we want to learn to live there and accept. If we learn ahead of time, if we have this teaching and through Color we've raised ourselves to the stature of accepting conditions as they truly are on that side and have the faith to stay on the Path long enough that the Path winds to the spiral of God's love, we have no difficulty in entering over there and just going on.

Treading a path of enlightenment is difficult here. But we're managing, aren't we, by going at night? Instead of lying in the Sleep World eased from all responsibility, we've accepted a responsibility to our very souls. We're taken to these temples. Each night has something we can bring back. It's true that many of us don't always bring them back, but if we would observe our lives closely enough we'd see the changes in ourselves.

These controls are the guideposts to the path. Try to think that in our dispositions and in living our lives, if you make a mistake of a bad temper once, you'll be tested three times. And it goes back to the cock crow: "Thou shalt deny me thrice before the cock crows." Denials are something that we must face, denials of things we desire. That's fine if we desire them and we produce them, but if we desire them and the other person is responsible, we're unhappy when they don't pan out. Then we're living the life of another person, and in our system of teaching, we believe that no human being has the right to play God in another's life.

We surely have to live with people, and go along with their plan of life as nearly as we can. So why don't we walk with, instead of against? We're trying to live the better life; why don't we just keep silent for a moment and see what comes through? There's where you tell the work from the temples. There's where you speak out loud what has been given you. There's that holding force. Feel yourself pulling down a beautiful curtain of cobalt blue just for a moment. Lift it and say what you want to say, but it will not be what you expected.

Because you've retired into the silence that has been created within you, the magnetic force of what God has given you as you walked and were taught in the temples. Here on earth we can go into churches and find a beautiful silence. As we partake of that communion, we're cleansed. That's very like the temples! Break thou the bread of life one with another, and in breaking it, give.

Try your colors! Tread that path of Color without anxiety. It's an easy path to learn. It's one that you can carry with you and be happy on it. For color is something that enlivens. Its environs are all about you, its beauty is manifold; it attracts the forces of light and understanding to you.

Color is a living thing, a force that God walks and talks in with his people. Once you have the faith to believe at every sunrise – and we've had some beautiful ones – every sunrise is another day, an opportunity to serve God and man. And with that thought in mind, there is a sunrise on the other side, a sunrise in glory that manifests itself to the degree that man is has developed and can recognize it. There is also the gentle fold of evening; there is noontime, the siesta of life, when those we love can come near; we're warmed by their love, and we know in truth, when we're there, that it is one world.

HELEN VON GEHR I was wondering if when you go on the spirit side of life, are you aware of the sun and the stars and the moon? And if so, do they have the same planetary effect?

MARY Yes. It's the same. It is very alike, but everything is more beautiful.

VIOLET In your description of morning when we were meeting the children, is that symbolic or real?

MARY That's real. Every morning, the children come up through that place.

*****

THE TEMPLE OF SPIRITUAL EXPRESSION

MIRIAM WIILIS Let us clothe ourselves in our keynote color, place the cloak of faith about our shoulders, and rest at ease in the body, that we may be free to breathe in this rarefied spirit of the living God. Breathe deeply and evenly until you are infilled in every cell of your body, in every spiritual center of your being, within the mind and the emotions, with the vibrant, vital life of the living, loving God. How wonderful it is that the uncreated spirit in the source of all power can focus down to us and feed us with the abundance of himself. This causes a wellspring of gratitude to rise in our hearts. Let it well up, bubble over, and be filled with glad thanksgiving. For this is God's gift, not only for our lives here, but for all life for eternity.

And so, as we learn this universal law of love, we can experience an integration throughout the whole of our life, and this brings heaven and earth together. This helps us to realize the silver lining behind the dark cloud, and the warmth of the sun of his love wherever we are, for he dwells in us. Let us bask in the greatness of this consciousness and truly lose ourselves in it, climb the Channel of our being toward the greater heights of wisdom, understanding, and fulfillment in our lives.

And to this end, let us stand on the lowest rung of the spiral of our being, in the color of the royal purple of faith, the unadulterated God power by which we step into the unknown, assured by faith that God power will sustain us and overcome our fears. We mount to the grey lavender of the holding force of patience, which we so need for balanced growth, and rise to the pink lavender of inspiration, uplifted and joyful. The rose lavender of the spiritual voice represents the light of conscience, the inner voice which reveals us to ourselves. The blue orchid of prophecy tells us what we may become, a foretelling, interpreting the revelation that comes as we listen to the inner voice.

The yellow bridge enlightens and lifts us to the rose orchid of the message bearer so that we can bring through the message from the higher dimensions, as the red lilac of the holding force for the band of teachers sustains the higher power, releasing earth's spiritual power to meet this higher power. Again, yellow's enlightenment uplifts us, this time to the glowing peach of the union of mind and spirit, creating a balance to free the intellect to become the recording instrument of the spirit.

The light blue orchid develops in us the spirit of brotherhood and brings the great invisible brotherhood to our consciousness. It awakens the love nature of humanity, the selfless love of the brotherhood of all humankind. The expression of this higher octave of love results in the blush orchid of serenity. With it self centeredness vanishes in the lightest green of desirelessness. Then is the rose bisque of grace a gift of God, his perfume. The light blue lavender of peace is the "peace that passeth all understanding." And here at the Fount of Supply, become conscious of this wonderful shower of the living God and all the vitality of it playing about you and infilling you.

HELEN VON GEHR I saw a symbol in meditation. It was as if there were a wall behind Miriam, and hanging from that wall was the picture you often see in Catholic homes of the Sacred Heart of Jesus. It almost looked like a bleeding heart.

MARY Well, we're approaching Good Friday. Spirit is showing us the great debt of love and the great life that was lived as a pattern for us, showing us how we can become, and to leave behind us the kind of vibration that other people can take hold of.

MIRIAM WILLIS Climbing the steep toward the Temple of Spiritual Expression, the challenge of merging is experienced in the soul and reflected to the mind in one's earth life. One may feel somewhat of a stranger to himself in this process. Such a change, however, spurs one on to greater reliance on the whisperings of spirit within, and a realization of a needed balance achieved by the merging of the three bodies.

As one approaches the Temple of Spiritual Expression, one sees an impressive forecourt of rainbow colors richly hued with twelve doors of flawlessly cut precious stones, clear and sparkling in the exquisite beauty of emerald, amethyst, ruby, sapphire, topaz and other priceless gems. One is attracted to his own door. As he passes through it he hears the cadences of his keynote and is arrayed in his keynote color. Paths and corridors are paved in the same precious stones as the door, converging toward the center into one vast temple, where the rainbow colored walls and roof form into a high dome. The colors become more delicate as they ascend and the whole emerges in the brilliant light of the opalescent Christ ray.

As one becomes accustomed to such brilliance, he realizes the presence of his Sponsor, high guides, and others in his Band or Order, and is given a panoramic view of the way in which they work to transmit divine power to the inspired seeker. One sees this channeled through man to earth in art, music, science, healing, prayer, writing, friendship, homemaking, business, protection, wisdom, love, joy, peace, harmony and brotherhood. We are wordless in profound silence, amazed at the immensity of detailed provision and heavenly service rendered by such multitudes of the humble great. Such is the selfless service of the life-giving source of supply, fulfilling the law of love.

One's whole being vibrates with desire to respond. No sooner does this yielding fill the soul than a chalice like a giant pearl lined with deep rose is in one's hand, and in silent awe one drinks of this loving cup. A great wave of power fills the vast area. Music is resounding everywhere, and one feels he will never doubt again nor withhold from expressing this generous supply of divine power that fills one to overflowing.

CLARA The top of the temple shone with a bright golden light extending like the rays of a star. Within the temple I was aware of being in a peach-yellow room with silk textured walls and a matching silk couch. I immediately felt surrounded by the glowing peach color of union of mind and spirit and felt total identification with my environment. I was examined and given aspects and promises of new chances to demonstrate my devotion to the Path. The contrast between those on the path and those who are not was made very clear to me, and the fact shown that it is not that anyone has been shortchanged, but that the majority has not yet claimed its heritage. It was also said that in youth one is often sustained by a dream, but later on it is inner development that allows one to make life into something where the quality will match that dream.

I was led into a room of topaz cut stone, the tones ranging from rich earth browns to amber to the yellow color of illumination. Here I was aware of our earth grounding in the physical relating to the higher life of the Planes, and had an enhanced understanding of all earth expression as representing something deeper and more penetrating than the limited mind can encompass. The substance of earth experience as revealed in this room had the quality of a shadow play, enactments of deeper truths and larger cosmic significance which were revealed. Even such small things as smiles, gestures, motions were shown in the light of their larger truth.

Later, outside the temple in the softness of a summer evening twilight, I looked out across an expanse of lawn and saw another temple ahead which seemed to beckon and offer the possibility of important answers. I felt a heightened sense of integration, as though a large body of work had been accomplished.

MARY   The seeker arrives at a mesa of universal consciousness. As he observes the sign posts, he reads "This way alone" and is given a vision nourished in the heart, as he begins using his intuition in the conquest of his emotional nature. Within the unused functions of your mind are dormant powers which can bring about a transformation of your life. We all have this path inside us. We yearn to express something greater than the world itself. Within us is the power to face life's difficulties, to harmonize our troubles and relationships. The masters have walked this path and we have followed in their footsteps.

Though many times those footsteps have been erased from our consciousness, we always feel the tread, and there are times when we know we've walked in the shoes of the master. We have accomplished something in this night work of ours. You who've been training in the temples know the developing power revealed in hunches and intuition as you seek to harmonize daily living with your keynote. Through this world at night, you found that teachers were willing to help you. Your answers may come when you least expect them.

MIRIAM WILLIS   Going to the many temples for soul training gives us a tremendous opportunity for spiritual expression. The training causes consciousness of this reality to well up from the soul to the mind more often, and to realize that it comes in so many different ways that we're sometimes slow to recognize the whisperings of spirit. In our moments of stillness above the limitation of thought, we can see the reality of the manifestation of growth in our lives.

As we reach a higher plane of spiritual awareness, we're challenged to live in that less dense atmosphere. Life must be lived in mental and emotional balance. It's in your silent attitudes; it's the thought of God in moments when you're alone; it's basic faith that carries you beyond the doorway of the material plane through the Channel of Color until you can prove the invisible becomes visible and the transmutation of all your development has become power motivated only by love. It's in the merging of the three bodies that the life force is expressed by spirit.

The ego reaching supreme God consciousness is only the beginning of divine unfoldment, because God consciousness reveals to the ego unending vistas, roads to travel in endless directions, but always onward to a higher, greater cosmic purpose. When physical beings traverse great stretches of history along the paths of evolution, the physical is percolating God consciousness through to higher mind strata.

VOLET   All human beings are mystics in some degree of development. What we need in treading this Eightfold Path is a change of heart, a change of mind. Our intent is waking up. Nobody can do it for us, but we're greatly helped on the other side, as well as by these heavenly etheric colors.

****

CHAPTER 6

THE TEMPLE OF SPIRITUAL SENSING

The stations on the steep to the Temple of Spiritual Sensing cause us to pause and take stock of our growth on the Path, to examine each one in the light of heightened understanding and its relationship to spiritual sensing. We begin with the knowledge that there's a physical counterpart to the spiritual life.

Yielding to Spirit is the keynote in all seven tests of the seven spiritual centers on the steep between the Temple of Spiritual Expression and the Temple of Spiritual Sensing. Through these tests, the centers are quickened into new life to a deeper and higher degree than ever before. This holds many a poignant relationship for the seeker. Through mirrored reflections, one is shown conditions that block sensitivity toward progression, and the seeker must become conscious of these in his daily living. He realizes that the use of Color will greatly help to develop these centers, and is grateful for the seven nights of discovery granted him.

MIRIAM WILLIS Clothed in the royal purple of faith, the seeker blindly feels his way onward, drawn by desire and the law of attraction. As he approaches the Temple of Spiritual Sensing, he enters an area of soft and foggy blue light. The temple is deep blue marble shot through with green at its foundations. The walls lighten gradually to the very palest lighter blue. There are seven arched doorways, and one is drawn to the door he most needs.

He enters through a Channel of Color and discovers it to be the reflection of his own Channel, which leads to a small chamber of uplifted consciousness, where he is encircled by beautiful colors of the Nile green of awareness, palest blue, rose lavender and orchid. He seems to float in these colors as one might in water, yet in this complete yielding, there is security. All spiritual centers are quickened into new life.

The seeker finds himself with many others in the temple itself. Color feeds and sustains us with the opaline blue of spiritual balance diffused with the rose orchid of the message bearer. Here the seeker becomes conscious of the reality of his inner sensing as the gateway, the entrée to the ultimate revealer of truth, wisdom and love.

MARY   As we're guided to this Temple of Spiritual Sensing, we realize all nature has given us a picture of the heaven world, a paradise. Woods, fields, valleys, hills, rivers and sea, clouds traveling across the sky, light and darkness, sun and stars, remind us heaven and earth are one and that our life is a gift of God. As we enter the temple, we see displayed in flaming letters, "Blaze love, destroy fear, banish hate, heal and reveal Christ's full power."

We saluted teachers who were sharing their illumination with us. We were asked to live within that light and radiate to all who were seeking development on the Eightfold Path. Filing into the temple's great hall, we hear these words: "Love is the coming to divine perfection of vision and inspiration, when the heart and soul sing praises. Love is the most sympathetic phase of energy. Love is wisdom so clearly penetrating in intensity that with unlimited power, it sweeps off the confines of experience and all obstructions. In each experience given you in these temples on the Planes, you as an evolving soul develop faculties and capacities, leaving less to be attained when you enter life eternal, giving you, the seeker, claim to celestial recompense.

We do know that each link that binds to the realms of sense must be severed. Higher consciousness isn't reached through reading books, but by stilling the senses and listening to the divine whispers of direction given to the soul. To sing the song divine is to transcend the realms of sense, to open the windows of the soul, and sense the stillness of true repose.

MIRIAM WILLIS   The aura is the area in which we sense. The study and practice of Creative Color causes the expansion of consciousness to experience spiritual sensing safely. Color is the path taught by Christ and by other great teachers. The knowledge of long lost color meanings revealed to our Mary and her development in the skill of using color are harmonious with what Jesus shared with the disciples.

VONNIE BRANCHFLOWER   I entered a small chapel at the foot of a mountain. Although I was with others, I felt alone on this journey. I knelt in prayer and meditation, thankful for guidance along the Path. A stream of light shone down around us in many beautiful colors, preparing us for the tests we would take on the upward climb.

As we spiraled up the mountain, the path became steeper. An orchard of many varieties of fruit was our first stopping place. Here our guides gave us fruit to taste, and we became aware that on Earth we would be receiving the fruits of the spirit. After clearing away negative dispositional characteristics which prevented our complete spiritual enjoyment, we were given a ripe olive. Tasting this, we began to see Christ as he had prayed in the Garden of Gethsemane, "Let this cup pass from me — yet not my will but thine be done." We understood something of the loneliness and disappointment in the weakness of his followers. Then a picture of our world today appeared, and the bitterness we tasted was most poignant.

We rededicated ourselves to the task of clearing away our transgressions. As the light of God's love poured down upon us, we followed that light along the path which led ever upward, with an awareness of an increased fragrance which we knew was a blessing from a test. Half way up the mountain, we came to another chapel. At first it seemed dark inside as we sat in prayer and meditation. Softly, we sang, "Open my eyes that I may see, open my ears that I may hear." At the close of the hymn we were each shown our blind spots. We saw loved ones, friends in many phases of our lives and adversaries in their true auric colors, and were told that while it might be difficult, our eyes could really be opened to new spiritual sight. We would have to see others through God's love. We were also enabled to hear the true heart's longing of all those who were there before us. The light blue orchid of brotherly love surrounded and enfolded us, and we went on with renewed faith.

Now the path was so rugged that to reach the top we clung close to the wall as we gained each new foothold, then reached down to help another up. Gaining the summit, we felt free of all that had hindered us along life's path. We were drawn toward a tall temple and entered a high roofed sanctuary through beautiful arched doorways where all was quiet and serene. We recognized teachers on the path as luminous light pulsated all about us. The Voice directed us to see the God light in all others.

LENORE   In this temple we were told of the importance of finding your own pattern for living, and how once this has happened, nothing is ever the same, because you know your importance in the kingdom. We were told that sensing leads to knowing. In empirical thought, one's physical senses give one what one accepts as truth. On the spiritual plane, the awakened higher senses lead to inner knowing. Dormant powers are roused through perseverance, through knocking on that door, and through your recognition of the answer. God speaks and manifests through his emissaries in all creation. As our sensitivity increases, we become ever more aware of how those on the unseen planes are constantly speaking to us and offering us truth.

We had a lesson in increasing insight, seeing into people and conditions, and were told that the degree to which we care about others is the greatest aid in our growth of this ability. As through love we give and receive, the sensing faculties are awakened and developed. In the sensing of one's own pattern and mission, we know the time allotted for this particular incarnation, and we know what we do with this time is our own free choice. At this point there came a definite renewal of purpose, a reaffirmation to grow and bring the light to others in the way we live, act and react.

In a circular domed room, blues and purples shot out in diamond shapes in a carnival of happy rays. We were told that the fruits were ripe for harvesting. Having grown in insight, the next step is acceptance, then to grow into what you've carved out for yourself, to recognize what has been added and finally to embrace it. There was exhilaration in the room with the feeling of being a new person, in accepting change and abiding in the newer, more beautiful version of the self.

Ephemeral colors surrounded us, binding us together in love. We know the inner mysteries will become simple truths living in our lives, truths that manifest into twelve pillars of wisdom. Regarding these twelve pillars, I was told there were twelve stations in the temple. The information I received is incomplete, but at the first station is the staff of life and the inscription: "I am the good shepherd. Love is at the end and the beginning and never ceases; it is eternal."

One station is a room the color of the 3rd of the Spiritual Arc of Blue, awareness of talents and source of power. Another station is a green room and another a pale peach room. The purpose of these stations is to clarify aspects of spiritual wisdom on the Eightfold Path.

******

THE TEMPLE OF WINGS OF ASPIRATION

The Temple of Wings comes after the Temple of Spiritual Sensing. It is situated on the steeps between the Temples of Spiritual Sensing and Spiritual Expansion. After having first been there the beginning of this week, we returned several times.

VIOLET In the Temple of Wings, we experience training in preparation for advancement, one of those things which you do singly with your high guide. An absorption of new power takes place in all areas of your life; spirit enters everywhere until the citadel of understanding powers reaches the summit of your development.

This temple is often known as the Temple of the Wings of Aspiration. It's likened to a butterfly having double wings, which signifies fourth dimensional thinking and is emblematic of balance and immortality. It speaks of life, love, light and power with each containing the other. Awe inspiring sounds emanate from within that impel the seeker to remove his shoes before entering.

LORNA LANE This temple design of a butterfly signifies immortality of the soul and spirit. Its expression is perfect balance, beauty and rhythm. It ties the soul into the great sweep of color rays, centralizing them into and by the spirit of God, the Creator.

VIOLET The butterfly design is interwoven with the cross, symbol of raising the soul of man to the stature and purity of divinity. The wings of the butterfly are fourfold, symbol of the foursquare or fourth dimensional, namely, the trinity and man. The first pair of wings stands for man, or earth life; the second for the Creator, or love; the third for the power of the Christ in man; the fourth for the inspirational uplift of the wings of spirit, or holy breath. The first spirals are life; the second spirals are love; the third spirals are light; and the fourth spirals are power. Each contains the other, blended in perfect balance, demonstrated through daily and hourly living becoming Christ Conscious.

Curves have no sharpness, only the sweep of rhythm, and the power of the continuing ray through the channel of consecrated living is an awakened soul. Balance is emphasized by the pair of wings and the surrounding circles on the butterfly's wings. The circles are symbols of perpetual protection and power of the expansion of immortal souls, immortality itself. The qualities of lightness, mobility and progression are symbolized by the wings.

The sweep, the curve, the spiraling into the center of the wings all show lessons to be learned on the 8th Plane, for their power, poise and wisdom illustrate truth that one is never outside or away from. The center of each wing or spiral is a vortex of concentrated color rays, and the tests we experience there are more searching. The rays referred to are the eight rays of the Eightfold Path: Ego, Healing, The Path, Devotion, Knowledge, Imagination, Discipleship, and Love.

HELEN MARSH Vertically, through the center of the butterfly, it's as if a mirror runs through the left wings or spirals of reality and are reflected in the right wings, as from a mirror, in exact duplication.

The reason for the inversion of the butterfly is to emphasize concern of the soul from itself to that of the thought and purpose of God, and of its usefulness through refinement and purity. The butterfly is inverted because it stands for the love offering of self continuously flowing Godward.

HANK The butterfly symbolically has no termination, but blends into eternity, into the ocean of love surrounding and penetrating life, light, love and power, because it is so manifested through these great primal rays of divinity and creation.

MARY We create our own conditions; we live in our own thinking, do we not? We create beauty around us, or we abhor the things we live with. Therefore, be creators under the wings of the Master. Create wings for yourself and go fly in Color. Spread your wings as the eagle of the morn. Kiss the sun of life, see where you can go and build a citadel of happiness, for joy should be in this world. The world is hungry and thirsty for the joy of living.

MIRIAM WILLIS   Shall we review the Eight Rays of the Eightfold Path?

RALPH   The First Ray or rung on life's ladder is attained by the recognition of one's Ego. We recognize this powerful ray through the thought and the magic of mind. The way to conquer failings of the individual soul is to drag them out into the light of pure reason and analyze them in their selfish and unselfish elements.

GLENN   The Second Ray of the Eightfold Path is Healing. One does not travel the path before one becomes the Way, the Path itself. Our task is to overcome the desire body. Faith that we can do so starts the healing process in our souls. Our emotions are lifted; we confront fear, hatred, greed, and the other lions that beleaguer us and we are able to overcome.

RUBY PERKINS   The Third Ray is called the Path. It stresses the practice of meditation and prayer. If we impartially review the facts of our life, we put away delusions and face life steadily. Eternity becomes the NOW.

FRED   The Fourth Ray of the Eightfold Path is Devotion. The Path becomes an adventure. In this ray, we raise the focus of our consciousness into the permanent physical atom, which in turn opens Cosmic Consciousness.

DORIS   The Fifth Ray is Knowledge. The tree of life is blossoming on the Path. As the ego expands in understanding, our physical senses are transcended through vision and our focus is raised to the permanent mental atom. Expanded consciousness brings true knowledge.

WILLARD   We call the Sixth Ray Imagination. This ray brings the realization of the Christ within, as the nervous system becomes like a high strung harp on which the breath of spirit plays. At this point, one is ready to receive spiritual sight and hearing.

DAN   Discipleship is the Seventh Ray of the Eightfold Path. When six are slain and laid at the Master's feet, the pupil is then merged into the Christ ray and lives therein. He has attained the power of the six previous rays. He has resolved past experiences in each of his bodies, into which his permanent atoms form a center. His night training with the invisibles is certain. On the 7th Ray, the seeker is open through the consciousness of all extended rays, and his life conforms to higher laws.

VIOLET   The Eighth Ray of the Eightfold Path is Love. Love never fails the disciple of Christ. The lamp he has lit cannot be hidden. At this point, he may go through a series of initiations. Only those who have tread this path are qualified to show the way. To this ray belong the great philosophic and scientific minds: the sages of India, Persia, Egypt, Greece and Rome all have had the powerful will to search the secrets of nature. It's said that "great as is the gulf between the good man and the sinner, it is greater between the good man and the man who has attained knowledge."

******

THE TEMPLE OF THE POMEGRANATE

The Pomegranate signifies wisdom and holiness. It contains 21 seeds and 21 elements. The Temple of the Pomegranate is formed into rooms like unto lotus leaves.

The two temples of Pomegranate and Wings of Aspiration are very much related and interwoven with their neighboring temples and thus become a subtle part of the teachings on the 8th Plane. Teachings from these temples are used as seeds for meditation.

FRED   Mary, how long a time in meditation do you recommend?

MARY I don't feel anyone needs to go into long meditation, nor do they need to do anything but be thankful to arise and face the newness of another day. Make it what you will. Watch exclaiming over things that displease you. Displeasure upsets the delicate colors of evolvement.

DAN   Are there any lions we need to be particularly aware of in this temple?

MARY   Criticism is a line of darkness that runs through the aura whenever a person takes away the other person's privileges of having their own right of opinion. When we're struggling so hard to become right ourselves, it's very easy to see the wrong in the other person. But who are we to judge whether a person is right or wrong when they go a different way than we do? The most poisonous thing that can interfere with development is criticism — criticism in any way.

And so I ask you to be careful what you say about others and to study the colors that come naturally. Use sympathetic understanding in place of criticism and you can bask in that, because you know you're doing the right thing. Use prayer. Prayer is something that just issues forth from a heart that's filled with love for humanity. It takes very little effort. A wordless prayer in Color goes out and sings its own song. It's a winged thing that touches the sick, the needy, anyone it's sent to. Cloak yourself in your keynote color and sound your keynote. They are your protection and your connection to the universal mind. And then, of course when a person gets to the place where they read auras, which many of you can do, you'll see the evidence. So let's take vanity and cut it out. Let's take egotism and banish it.

I came to Earth for a purpose—have I grasped what I came for? Have I used all of my talents? The story of the talents is quite plain to me as I read them, as Christ told of them. And so, how many talents did we come with? What are we going to present as treasure when we go back? I believe there are some people who are extremely talented, but who either withdraw through fear or lack of faith. There is great beauty and talent lying dormant within; there are unused chambers of the mind. That mind has much to give, even as we go along day after day regretting that we're not like our brother or sister or someone else.

We can be enlivened to the peace that lies beyond us. When we enter that isle of peace, we come back with pictures given us in dreams and visions. All are a part of that inner you. All that you are can be expressed through faith and understanding.

And if you're able to take away the fear of death in just a few people with the idea, "When I graduate I'll go on into a greater world. I know I'm accountable for every act that has wronged another person or myself, and there's always time to work on past misunderstanding."

Death to many people is darkness. Death is life to me. I teach it, as I love to think it. But if I heard of the death of one of you, don't think I wouldn't grieve because I would no longer be able to see you on Earth and associate with you here again. I would have to adjust, would I not? Love has cause for sorrow. And so, I never criticize a person when they say, "Oh, I'm so lonely; I've lost my dear one." Of course they're lonely! That's love. That's the other half of love, for love has many facets.

Jesus wept. And if one so great as he could shed a tear for humanity, imagine what we should be shedding now! And so let us watch, wait, look and listen for signs, changes that will come upon us, for people in our midst, people we don't expect to turn spiritually will turn. And oh, the atmosphere that one lives in when they know that you can live in immortality now!

"For where I am, there shall ye be also."

****

THE TEMPLE OF SPIRITUAL EXPANSION

As one travels the Path earnestly seeking, there are many new experiences along the way of spiritual unfoldment and expansion. This is a climbing process and a spiritual centering to the one spirit within. The temple is the temple within, the uppermost peak, the blending of all the highest in spiritual achievement. It becomes the color hoped for, the Christ ray. This color comes from the Spiritual Arc of Yellow. It is the 11th color of the Arc, meaning unifying the self with the Christ within.

MIRIAM WILLIS Growth is the keynote of the seven tests on the steep one climbs to the Temple of Spiritual Expansion. Spiritual food, rest, and exercise comprise the pattern of the tests we experience here. Each soul receives that which he particularly needs, much as a seed draws to itself the elements in the soil which nurture it to maturity.

The attraction in the climb toward the temple is strongly magnetic, for sensing seems to lure one through its ephemeral vagueness to follow its lead in faith and hope to clearer fulfillment. One's powers are tested here and the muscles of the soul are strengthened thereby. This is a joyous way, full of song and laughter dappled with the sunlight of illumination and the cool shade of deep silence in the quiet resting places.

In this temple we enter a powerful divine force of light in which the strength of each becomes the strength of all. We're one with the Father. There alone is secret achievement, joy all abiding, and we know we live encompassed with the great cloud of witnesses and invisible helpers. Herein is peace attained that is the inflorescence of courage, wisdom and love. Here we experience a state of the most intense illumination.

This is the secret of development; it's the mystery of redemption. And as we go along, we have confidence that the moments of illumination have been the stepping stones toward a further expansion of being. We see whether or not the memory referred to as the God within will be quickened to give to each of us a link of progression in the height of illumination, as we now think of the Temple of Spiritual Expansion.

It's always helped me to realize the logic of the continuity with which God deals with us as we grow and climb. It's like an unbroken pillar of light within that grows more brilliant and reflects more often through our memory to our conscious mind. Then we find that the heavenly power which reaches down and infills us through our night training becomes more unified, like the glowing peach color of the union of mind and spirit in the Channel of our being. And we find that our prayers reach farther.

What is this but an expansion of spiritual growth? You've had flashes as you've prayed for people when you suddenly see them, sense them, feel them. You pray and the vibration on which you ride, your colors flow to the person, and you feel the difference, don't you? Isn't this an extension, an expansion of spirit within us? Perhaps each one of us can realize this with a greater continuity of growth than we have before if we just expect the expansion of consciousness to increase.

MARY   We were put to the test of going to the Temple of Spiritual Expansion, and many of us did not pass our test there because of having too many doubts and fears. To believe is still to doubt.

As we looked into this temple this week, I noticed things I hadn't noted before. As we grow each time as we go to the temples, we're ever learning, ever expanding. Everything is a circle in this great Temple of Spiritual Expansion, the circle being a prominent symbol, and we know its meaning is wholeness, infinity, no beginning and no end. The circle naturally expands because we only realize a half circle as we see the earth. But if we see it's one world without end amen, the glorious amen is a true circle.

JOHN BASINSKI The Möbius strip again ... the inner becomes the outer and the outer becomes the inner.

MARY This is a very important temple, and I was happy that you were even in the courtyard. Sometimes we have to seek to bring something out; we have to search for the words of expansion. And as our consciousness picks it up, within ourselves we have gone into the field of memory. Therefore, this past week, our field of memory has been awakened and expanded.

VIOLET I saw small round pools in expanding rows that when looked at formed a large, fan-like shape, the narrow end toward the temple. They blazed out in beauty, each pool having a different coloring. Then as if one had picked up the shadings from the water, these many colors were in the building itself in patterned form. All across the façade were round sections giving forth gem-like brightness. It was hard to tell of what the colored sections were composed. They appeared to be enamel about three feet in circumference, set in bands. The background was of a soft cream color. There were towers reaching up to quite a height that were constructed with balconies ending in spires. I counted twelve of these. The whole emphasis of the Temple of Spiritual Expansion is sending forth, as Christ did his disciples.

In this temple each one experienced an intense deepening of their belief in God the Father through Jesus the Christ. And this took the form of encountering suggestions of unbelief, so that for each there had to be formed a positively embraced reaction. In this manner, one came to the full realization of that which to them had become knowing. It wasn't hoping; it was a deep certainty of belief augmented here in the atmosphere of beauty, harmony and color; it became fact, certainty, something so sure that it could be carried out to others.

JEANNE I was aware of working on my lions this week on the Other Side. I approached the temple, the forecourt of which seemed made of glass reflecting many colors. The tapered columns resembled icicles, their designs of transparent geometric patterns of crystal or icy glass appearing jewel-like when reflecting lights from the sun. Inside the temple, I found myself in a room with several doors and heavy walls. I was aware of having to do things that I have resisted in my growth until now. I had the distinct feeling of one part of me pulling the other against the will of that lazy, lethargic other part, taking me into areas I have either postponed or neglected, or to areas in which the dust has been swept under the rug.

It was no longer possible to avoid these things, and I was made to face them in my night work this week. I was taken to a tower of gold in which I soared to the top and was given a grainy earth-brown substance to take back with me to my physical life. Try to take a larger view, I was told, to see all the troublesome things in a larger framework, thereby diminishing the importance of hurts and scars, in an expanding horizon of comprehension as to the ultimate significance of earth lessons.

I was given a test on tact with Margaret. Then I was shown a series of square blocks, each one part of a whole, having their basis in common stuff, yet each a separate unit. The common ground was made clear to my consciousness in a lesson of further reaching to step into the other person's sandals, seeing another's point of view, and walking in love.

I was shown the need for forgiveness and perspective of gratitude for what one has been blessed with, and given further enlightenment on how the soul attracts what is best for its growth. I was tested on the lions of resentment and jealousy, and there was a massive clearance in my subconscious on fear and on blaming others for my own mistakes. I was shown how in the sour areas, there is the help and constant filling with light and understanding by our guides in the temples at night.

I had a lesson on maintaining inner calm, and was given an extra supply of the grey lavender of the holding force of patience. I was told I would need this quality a good deal in the next few weeks in my earth life, and the keynote given me all week long in every possible channel from the other side, born out in my earth existence, has seemed to be change, steadied by the holding force of patience.

I was given a water test pertaining to fear and insecurity. This was to help center the self; one establishes a safe center in the world with which one is familiar, yet there are deeper areas which one lets slide.

My own areas in this sense were pointed out to me very clearly this week, areas long hidden, buried perhaps years ago yet nevertheless still plaguing my subconscious, needing to be recognized, faced and dealt with. There is a greater security to be had, a far stronger center to be found, not just the force of habit acceptance of a pattern with which one has become comfortable over the years, nor the naive surface kind of emotional faith, but a positive force of a much deeper kind of balance.

In the water test I tried to take the easy way (through fear of the harder path, afraid I would drown), and to my surprise found the so-called easy way was in reality the hard way. I was shown very clearly how the old way had to be overcome for new and more daring vistas to be reached.

One night after a test of extreme fear, a teacher in a pale magnolia-colored robe came to my side, held my hand and comforted me. I reached out one of my hands to his and felt his touch. With my other hand I reached up to feel his face. This was at the end of the night's session, and I was coming back to my body. For a brief instant I hovered between the two worlds, then I opened my physical eyes, saw that I was back in my bed, yet I still felt the touch of the teacher very strongly to the extent that my hands were bent to the shape to accommodate his form, and my senses contained the feeling of his body. It was an ephemeral moment, but one of strong reality and beauty. The next day in a message, the teacher gave me his name as Anamander, a Greek, of the Band of Apollo.

MARGARET First we seemed to be having a "meal of peace," which I interpret to mean we attended a communion service for peace. We then were in a temple with a domed roof of soft gold. The roof was suddenly rent, admitting a bright shaft of the light of the 12th color of the Spiritual Arc of Blue, the light iridescent sky blue of fourth dimensional consciousness and the realization of man as a spiritual being.

There followed a lesson in color. Then we came to a vividly white step with clouds of silvered lavender at the sides. All about us was silver bell music. The silvered sound and color with the billowy lavender substance make the loveliest sound and sight I can imagine at the moment. Above, the sky is a very bright blue. Enraptured by the bell tones, I nearly miss seeing a tall golden harp against a magnificent golden pink background.

Words come: "Let the winds of longings be attuned to the harps of heavenly desiring that the breath of angels may set a-quiver strings and make the plan of a heavenly choir."

Those harps again! Indicative of the 8th Plane and the Eightfold Path. There followed several paragraphs in the same vein, ending with the injunction to "patrol the dawn's emerging line as sentry of the view that brings the morn." I hear the stars singing a farewell song just before the dawn, as if the stars, giving so much light with their sparkle, they actually sing in the day as a salute to the rising sun. I feel that such glory would be possible only if all the galaxies should combine to make such a showing. I feel that if my ears were only bright enough I could hear the stars converse and hear the plans they have in store for earth.

I was given a poem. At the close of the poem there was a flash of glowing pink lavender of inspiration combined with a warm, peachy apricot. I saw a glimpse of a few silvered lavender pillars connected by delicate ribbed vaulting. Next, I see a river in light, opalescent colors, which flows both upstream and down. The current carrying the upstream portion is a very pale clear blue. I am suspended above the middle, looking upstream. Beyond the source, over the horizon, is a brilliant pale gold light.

Next, I'm in a tall ceilinged room facing a large, curved window watching a weighing device for measuring the motes that gleam on sunbeams. The motes were making a pattern in rich golds, beiges and browns of varying hues. There were patterns of light of various shapes hung perpendicularly, acting as huge filters. I thought at first that there was to be a general lesson on life structure, then it seemed to pertain to my own life structure.

It was as if I could see the residual of all the past lifetimes in symbolic form. Gradually I perceived an intricate structure emerge. Depth of vision, of pattern, and many dimensions are now possible. Next came a lesson in perspective; then one in music; then very excellent help with interpreting my son's music. I saw Violet in the life structure room.

CLARA I was first aware of a white wall with bright, rose colored flowers against it. As I walked along the wall into darker areas, I saw night blooming jasmines on the other side. As I stepped inside into the darkness, there was a flaming light composing a beautiful man's face, with hair swept upward, aflame. This face seemed to be over a pool. I entered the water and floated face up.

As I stepped out, the water just flowed off, leaving me perfectly dry. My white gown was made of many layers of thin material. I stepped down onto a walk around the pool and then stopped to look into another deep pond of reflecting green blues. I was next aware of walking with many people in white on a long, diagonal road. We were walking slowly.

Ahead there seemed to be an area with a huge stone barrier like the inside of a planetarium. Once we reached this area I found there were no walls or ceilings. I am acutely aware of the brightness of the stars and the depth of the skies. I feel wonder at the magnitude and totality of all distances and a closeness to all things, a part of all.

ALMA JOHNSON I saw myself with some members of the group, and I was wearing cobalt blue. And from what I heard, I probably needed it.

MARY I think there was one time that we all wore blue as basic relief, and a release from all the powerful rays that we walked through as we witnessed the dawn and the sunset and we walked through the radiance of that, and I believe each one of us put on cobalt blue. You remembered that.

VIRGINIA LOCKWOOD I was told, "Go in the door of City Hall," and so I did. This building was extremely modern, all glass with white framework, and huge. I said I must go in the front door and turn around to the left, and there would be something I wanted there. Immediately Mary in her radiant form was there. She was shaking her finger at me, and she said, "Now you must go around to the side -- there's what you want."

MARY I think I'd seek more on that, dear, because you didn't get enough, and I think you can get more.

HELEN VON GEHR Water seems to be such a predominant thing this week, and circles, too. My first vision was of a figure holding up a round, flat thing like a bird bath feeder that was lined with flowers with water pouring out of it. I could see this figure rise up, and then a little bird came and perched on the thing.

LENORE Last week I dreamed of purple. I dreamed that there was a birthday party for me. I was saying, "It's been many years since I had a birthday party—since I was a child, in fact, so I wondered if maybe I was having a spiritual birthday. And so I was led through a house containing all the people who came to the party. In each room there was a round table, and there were slices of bread on all the tables. After that, I went into another room where there was a young woman in birth travail, very near the birth of the baby. It seemed almost as though I could be a midwife and deliver this baby. Then the next night I did see a baby in my dream. I had a strong baby boy.

MARY In symbology, any young thing usually has something to do with development if you're in spiritual work.

MIRIAM WILLIS Appearing as a sunrise heralding the dawn, the Temple of Spiritual Expansion is glimpsed on the crest of a hill towering above the treetops and surrounded by a multitude of fragrant flowers watered by cool fountains, tinkling waterfalls, and streamlets of bluest water. The temple itself is like a glorious sunrise. At first one wonders whether its light emanates from its own glory or is a reflection of the rising sun, and one is attracted to investigate. The temple seems to be posited in the grey-green of basic understanding, of variegated marble shot through with the nile green of awareness.

Many turrets of great height surmount it. The color above the nile green is the pale lettuce green of desirelessness that gradually changes into warmer tones of yellow, gold and peach, blue, rose, lavender and the whole gamut of multitudinous pastel tints, most glorious to behold. Each entrance seems to be guarded by an angel of light, and as one enters the temple, one is filled with an almost floating sensation of lightness and weightlessness.

The atmosphere is delicately fragrant. Despite the outside turrets, inside there seems to be no roof – in fact, no enclosure, just great expansion. One feels an identification with this expansion, a power that no materiality can limit, for its light and substance pass through it, so refined is its essence, so powerful its gentleness, so secure its balance. One is not oneself and yet one is identified with a greatness which has heretofore been beyond one. The vastness without now seems to be within. Through this metamorphosis of spiritual expansion, one is poignantly conscious of the timelessness of spiritual growth.

MARY Upon entering the gates of this temple, we saw a splendid vision. Above the gates, glowing in great letters, it reads: "From my mind, I remove the last vestige of doubt." All appeared new and strange, yet inexpressibly rare and beautiful. The trees, when I first saw them in their incredible greenery, ravished and transported me. Their sweetness and unusual beauty made my heart leap with ecstasy. Then with the thought of Earth came the sense of everyday life. But the true mystic sees right through to the core of things and sees our world as God fashioned it. He sees through all those layers of doubt to the radiant heart of man.

The great teachers tell us the good things we dream of are realities quite as demonstrable as the celestial bodies whose light reaches us across unthinkable miles of space. The teachers tell us, "When the seeker becomes aware of expanded consciousness, he will be keyed to the highest truth his spirit knows, and those obstacles are no longer a part of his life; instead, his life's pattern will possess him, and achievement is his. He need only to believe and have the courage to claim his birthright."

Sometimes our memory, in a mellow and brooding mood of detachment and awareness of God's gift to our lives, causes us to accept its truth. We do at times look back and suddenly perceive beauty where before all was chaotic. Again we ask, "What is this thing called memory?" Immediately the answer comes, "It is God in us."

The point I wish to make is: why not anticipate memory, which shows all things in their hidden beauty, and declare now in the present moment, "I will have faith." And though it is only a flash of unexpected "seeing," it lets us perform a miracle and allow spirit to transform our lives. So walk on, dear ones, on Christ's radiant way. And why shouldn't we literally scintillate with life that God is pouring into us every moment day and night? For are you not his shining substance, his rainbow of promise? Your creation remains a miracle.

WILLARD   In the Temple of Spiritual Expansion, we experienced an intense deepening of faith in God, our source, and the path of love taught by Jesus the Christ. In our tests, we encountered suggestions of unbelief and our reaction was a full realization of that which to us was "knowing"-- not hoping, but deep certainty of conviction. I was aware of my need to practice right view and right action.

MARY At the moment in life when silence enfolds you, think of the invisible hosts who love you and are willing to be a part of that silence. With all that counts against us, more than anything else is the discontented mind that is continually analyzing conditions about one. The man is wise who can work with both the visible and the invisible, then depart from all and come down to do the simple things of everyday life in a joyous mood.

******

CHAPTER 7

THE TEMPLE OF SPIRITUAL IMAGINATION

MIRIAM WILLIS Seven stations on the steep were presented before for our communion. The tests on the steep between the Temple of Spiritual Expansion and the Temple of Spiritual Imagination require faith, for Spiritual Expansion knows no end, and in truth has no beginning; it is an eternal cycle into which one enters and proceeds to become more familiar with as one is attuned to the eight rays of the Eightfold Path. The seven spiritual centers are quickened, and much as the sun's warmth and attraction cause plants to respond to the chemical changes in their growth, so must the qualities and character of the rays Eightfold become incorporated in our being, thus creating chemical changes in our nature.

MARY Lest we become impatient with seeming repetition, remember: we're growing and expanding in consciousness. Can we view these stations in a new light? As we enter each station let us clear our consciousness of any old trappings related to words and enter the silence, where our soul can remind us of the growth we have attained. Are we open to the new? Have we discarded the old? Let us go within, approach each station and listen.

Many scenes enter our consciousness, and we realize that truth unfolds through spiritual imagination clothed in symbols, which with the development of this faculty we are able to interpret. To man's awakened Christ Consciousness, he knows that spiritual imagination is the oracle of truth, truth concerning his whole universe insofar as his development is able to embrace it. It takes the sun of spiritual imagination to grow a seed.

We plant a thought which is like a seed. And by faith, the seed grows as we nurture it. Then as the seed blossoms, its fragrance comes to us and is expressed through our life. We give it out to other people as the aroma of our life.

MIRIAM WILLIS We know that spiritual imagination is the oracle of truth concerning ourselves and our whole universe.

MARY The Temple of Spiritual Imagination covers a vast area. It seems almost like a city, with a translucent wall of the grey lavender of the holding force of patience enveloping it like a cloud so ethereal one can see multitudinous colors through its veil. As one passes through this ephemeral substance, it seems to enfold one in suspended security.

The temple is as the hub of a great wheel, the spokes or divisions of which swirl upward in a spiral from its deep blue-violet foundation to a vast gamut of kaleidoscopic colors too numerous to define. The filmy grey lavender changes into an overlay of lighter tints of iridescent mother of pearl as it ascends.

ANDREW It's interesting you mention the great wheel and its spokes. This reminds us of the spokes of the wheel of life of the Eightfold Path, the eight spokes representing the eight elements of the path.

MARGARET We relate these spokes to the eight rays of the Eightfold Path: Ego, Healing, the Path, Devotion, Knowledge, Imagination, Discipleship and Love.

DAN I distinctly recall that right view, right aspiration, right speech, right action, right livelihood, right effort, right mindfulness, and right concentration were emphasized in temple lectures this week.

MIRIAM WILLIS The whole temple, intricately carved and bejeweled, is glorious to behold. In this temple one is trained to realize that all the spiritual senses are fed and enlivened by the power of spiritual imagination. When powers are sufficiently developed, one becomes keenly aware of the Christ within and of becoming "as a high-strung harp upon which the breath of spirit plays."

MARGARET As Miriam mentioned, the Sixth Ray of the Eightfold Path, Imagination, was particularly emphasized. I recall hearing that ray ringing in sonorous tones.

JANE I've had so many unexpected insights and recollections in the halls of remembrance in the different temples that house memories, especially including this week's Temple of Spiritual Imagination. To put in perspective everything I've been shown is a challenge. Although I've achieved as much understanding as I'm capable of, regarding overall coherence, I still see "through a glass darkly," and I'm waiting for the "face to face" ... an aha moment. My lions continue being revealed. They're sometimes hard to accept. I long for fuller clarity as I confront these inescapable, troublesome flaws and I sometimes want to revolt. This week I was confronted with lions involving the desire to control, exemplified in impatience leading to anger.

RICHARD One finds having visited the Temple of Spiritual Imagination has quickened his spirit of adventure, opening so many doors through which one had long wished to enter. This requires an increase of Channel power, which grows as one uses it. We're reminded that divine imagination is the fruit of the Eightfold Path.

******

THE TEMPLE OF BALANCED FAITH

BERNARD BURRY On the steep to the Temple of Balanced Faith, we're given the opportunity to reexamine important concepts touching on balanced faith as it applies to ourselves. At this stage on the Path can we ask: where am I in the development of my life? How has my balanced faith been expanded, or has it?

LOLA After leaving the Temple of Spiritual Imagination, new power within became increasingly evident, as did the need for it. There was a buoyancy in being carried on the wings of morning with the eagerness of moving forward to new and wonderful experiences. A teacher along the path said, "Clothe yourself in your keynote color," so I wrapped my color of purple with rose about me and found myself before a beautiful temple.

ANDREW The power of the Spirit of God will reveal itself to every sincere seeker of the path, who by faith recognizes the power of divinity within. No great enlightenment can become evident in your life without faith. If you once become aware of the plan for your life, you will know nothing can stand in the way of your search for development, nothing can mar your understanding. The seeker gladly accepts the law: man himself is the atomic miracle.

119

JEANNE I was shown the need for clearing worry and anxiety in order to practice right mindfulness and right concentration. Behind a door done in tapestry, the 7th color of the Spiritual Arc of Purple, the brilliant rose fuchsia of sympathetic understanding predominating, I was shown memories of childhood and allowed to relive the qualities of faith of my early years. Behind yet another door, I was given added discrimination and discernment in order to improve my judgment and avoid efforts wasted on useless ventures in the future. Right view came more into focus.

I saw how color has increased my faith. For each problem being worked on, I was taken into another area and fed the colors I needed. One large area maintained an atmosphere of the 9th color of the Spiritual Arc of Red, alternating light rose and light blue stripes, meaning selflessness, overcoming bigotry, developing on the Path, and consciously living in the Presence. I was then fed a giant dose of the 10th spiritual color of the Arc of Red: coral rose with a flesh pink center, meaning a nature resplendent in warmth and kindness, considerate and thoughtful, with a talent for bringing out the best in others; followed by all twelve rays of the Spiritual Arc of Purple, spiritual balance. I felt myself as a sponge absorbing vital energies.

Other areas of the temple visited include: a purple velvet chamber, the texture of which seemed to penetrate my whole being, an enclave type of hall where the words, "Not my will but thine" appeared, and a white marble esplanade. Then, clothed in my keynote color of alice blue, I mounted a staircase of greyed pink lavender, the color of harmony, for a fire test.

The room was roofless and large, of a pale color with gold fixtures and a white marble floor that had a discernable pattern of alternating triangles and pentagrams. My guide took my hand, asking if I were ready. A ring of fire had been placed about the floor, the flames burning low. As I stepped upon the coals to walk the circle, the flames leapt higher, but did not touch me. Underneath, my feet felt cool, and I knew I had protection. The fire, I knew, burned more inwardly than without, and after I had walked the entire circles, the teacher told me I had passed a test of faith.

VIOLET   On the approach to the Temple of Balanced Faith, I learned that one of the major lessons in this temple is poise, and how in one's life poise can be gained. The structure of the temple is most interesting, for it is very varied in its different parts and forms; these are placed in such perfect balance that they seem necessary one to another, and the total effect is beauty and grace.

VIRGINIA ANDERSON   You know that the floor pattern that Jeanne described tonight in her report, I was there last night with so many of you. It was a very etheric atmosphere, but the outstanding thing was the teachers among us who were wearing the colors that both Sylvia and Patti are wearing tonight, only brocaded with more gold in the flowers to the hip. They also wore a cap which was that same vivid electric blue, and the top of the cap was triangular.

ESTHER BARNES   Two separate wings emanate from one common entry. The Temple is engulfed in flowered beauty, steeped in subtle truths and crowned with poise, maintaining the spirit of balance both within and without. Within its spacious halls and assembly rooms, color breathes in rhythmic vibration.

It is twilight and there's a hush over all. A slight stirring of rustling leaves and faintly twittering birds are heard as one drinks in the stillness. Then twilight is overtaken by growing light and the surroundings become clearer. There's a feeling of peace and freedom, as though being enfolded in endless trust and security. We're tempted to stay here forever in utter contentment, but as the power of faith builds within, we're filled with an urge to go farther and to press on along the many narrow, winding paths. In the growing light we encounter many fellow travelers on the path. Each is alone with scarcely enough room to place his feet. As our paths ascend, the climb requires all one's effort. A rod and staff are given each seeker with the words, "Lean on hope and trust and go forward in faith." This moves aside any brambles and stones that threaten. As we proceed, the path becomes wider and less impeded, and we discover increased faith as we persevere.

Suddenly, simultaneously, we all burst into song, each person singing in his own keynote. The tones blend in perfect harmony and cast colored lights enveloping all in soft rainbows. We walk through these colors and see that we've reached the summit of a height on whose crest we see the Temple of Balanced Faith.

The temple is like a gigantic bird poised in balance above the nest of promised fulfillment. The wings are spread wide, bathed in all shades of purple, violet, fuchsia and orchid. This fantastic achievement in architecture seems perfectly natural, and we find ourselves in the nest secure and happy, protected by the balanced wings of faith. Born within the soul is a knowing faith, a realization that God's revealed plan for one's life can be fulfilled.

MIRIAM WILLIS   As the seeker proceeds up the steeps of seven tests, he discovers the difference between his mental imagination and divine imagination. He realizes he must leave the comfort of the mental body and rise into the vastness of the seeming nothingness of higher faith. Like the young bird, he finds he must return to the security of the nest, his mental habitat.

Each time he ventures forth he grows in strength, and through trial and error he learns to trust the higher flight that opens to him the vast horizons of the heaven world and clothes reality in symbolic pictures which he gradually learns to interpret. This discernment requires training, and it is with relief that one finds a resting place in the beautiful gardens surrounding the Temple of Balanced Faith, where one rests as a traveler might on coming home from a long trip filled with many wonders.

The reason we find ourselves challenged by every sort of problem is because the spirit in man demands materials to try its strength. Spirit is a force so powerful that it tests us with problems that require solving in new ways, not by the outmoded techniques that once satisfied the soul. Spirit becomes a force of creative energy to acquire a fresh concept of what it means to be a spiritual unit in the Kingdom.

One of the lessons learned in the Temple of Balanced Faith is poise and how it can be gained. As many aspects of self are revealed, one is shown the need for clearing worry and anxiety. Sympathetic understanding is a valued aspect of balanced faith. It involves heart and mind working together to offer uplift to another who is distressed. Sympathetic understanding, the 7th color of the

Spiritual Arc of Purple, brilliant rose fuchsia, is closely related to compassion. There's love in this activating color as well as clear thinking, faith, intelligence and deep feeling.

The Temple of Balanced Faith is one of the major temples in the progression of our spiritual ongoing, where faith is strengthened and developed. Expressing faith, one earns the right to explore and discover treasures in the vast areas of the wings, body and head of this great bird like edifice. Again and again we return for the protection of the temple's balancing force.

FRANK   Faith enters into all phases of life. Most potent of forces, constantly flowing God power, whether realized or unrealized, is available to all mankind. Faith is a driving force with unlimited possibilities.

VIOLET The Eight Rays of the 8th Plane are once again strongly emphasized: Ego, Healing, the Path, Devotion, Knowledge, Imagination, Discipleship and Love. Regarding these, I received this in the temple: we're constantly working on the Ego; we receive many Healings in the temples of the 8th Plane; we're on the Path and we ARE the Path; Devotion is called upon to travel this Path; we gain Knowledge on the Path; we use Imagination to go farther on the Path; Discipleship and Love are the attainments and the blessings of the Eightfold Path.

MARY The seeker realizes that harmonic response to the individual life might well be named "the color scheme," as color gives expression to that which lends warmth, beauty, and illumination to life's path, easing otherwise hard traveling, transforming the iron chain of obligation into the sparkling, bejeweled golden thread of privilege. May the purple robe of faith envelope you in your daily needs. Bless you.

Father in Heaven, we come to thee seeking our way through the darkness of not understanding. Give us understanding hearts and minds to receive. Enlighten us with the wisdom of those that help us. And in the Name of Jesus Christ, give us happiness and let us know the meaning of love. For health and healing we ask thee, oh Christ. Amen.

******

THE TEMPLE OF ENLIGHTENMENT

MIRIAM WILLIS   The steeps leading to the Temple of Enlightenment are filled with the reward of one's testings, and here understanding is greatly enlightened. One is conscious of a most rarefied atmosphere filling his whole being with new life. Every sense is quickened to a new rhythm. The seeker becomes aware of the rarefied beauty of trees, of cool waterways, of tender green meadows, flower-strewn and soft beneath his feet. All this is overcast by a delicate pink glow in the landscape's atmosphere. At times the seeker is lifted by the gentle wind of spirit and carried swiftly to the station of his next test, where in the enlightenment thus gained, he sees more clearly his responsibility and how to fulfill it. The choice is always his. Inevitably, this manifests in his earth life as well.

We enter the court of the Temple of Enlightenment, where we are charged with more enabling power to travel back and forth over the steeps of testing. The Temple of Enlightenment is so brilliant that one sees it at first only as a great sunburst of light. As one's eyes are able to receive it, one sees an edifice of alabaster, pure golden yellow with rose and peach to palest breath of yellow as it reaches high into the heavens and becomes formless in the brilliant light. Its doors are simple, dignified arches with single words emblazoned in light over them, words such as simplicity, truth, sincerity, justice, purity, trust, love.

Each door leads into a corridor of increasing light, until one sees oneself clearly reflected, and in this enlightenment sees one's lacks and attainments revealed according to the depth and height of the soul's development.

Having viewed himself thus, one passes through the veil of light for further initiation into a greater degree of enlightenment. Within this veil, he is enveloped in many colors according to the need these colors represent. He applies these as he emerges through a lighted color bath initiation. His sponsor and others bless him, and he joins with many fellow seekers in a great spiraled circle. Silence fills the rapt throng, as the great Voice speaks. The words I heard were: "Enlightenment is the reward of soul expansion and balanced faith. Walk in light and your feet will not stumble."

MARY Through silence, the creator of balanced faith, we're led into the Temple of Enlightenment. As we progress through this mystic temple, we realize faith through silence and meditation is the awakening of the soul. There passes not a day but the soul adds ever widening domain where faith brings man nearer to his invisible self and takes a greater part in all his actions.

A mysterious brotherhood must have been left by the great master, the Christ, that calls man's soul out of the silence to follow the path of enlightenment which draws men nearer to their brothers. We find a great desire for knowledge and understanding, conscious that within our soul dwells an imperishable power walking by our side in everyday life.

Does it not seem as though the supreme cry of the soul would pierce the dense clouds of doubt that envelop man, could he but hear the call? However great the soul, it was not intended to wander in isolation through space and time unaided. When the spiritual sea is storm-tossed and its whole surface troubled, then is the moment ripe for Christ Consciousness to impress upon the soul of the seeker, even if it be only in the briefest vision or dream, the sensing of Christ's presence or his voice in the temple.

A Swiss inscription says, "Speech is silver, silence is golden." I believe speech is time, silence is eternity. Bees cannot work except in darkness of the hive. Thought works best through silence. Prayer is the means by which we actually raise our own vibrations to more nearly match the divine.

As we climb the planes and steeps of Heaven, we discover more and more that each temple is distinct in style and purpose. This Temple of Enlightenment is no exception. The approach to it is somewhat clouded as to enhance it's domed form. There is no lack of nature's beauty here. The music of songbirds and the perfume of flowers laden the air. There are lofty arches formed of alabaster in the corridors and naves steeped in color and design. Ethereal are the assembly rooms bathed in brilliant lights, calling attention to the temple's scope and purpose, which has to do with plans for the soul and how it must be nourished and fully understood. Here there is recognition of the soul's cry for expression and worthiness.

Enlightenment, so essential to growth and progression, is based upon activated prayer, meditation and the therapy of thoughtful silence. Gratitude opens the door to further enlightenment: gratitude for the training and the heavenly teachers who train. Surround yourself with the rose peach color of gratitude. Bless you.

PATTI I saw our group traversing a long narrow white walkway surrounded with bushes and trees with fragrant white blossoms. It was a very serene setting. Lights spaced about three feet apart made the area even more luminous. We passed fountains and ponds, spacious grounds, and a pretty circle of yellow flowers. We then stood facing the temple, which is set inside a gate, large and creamy yellow in color. Up close there was an inlaid floral design that looked as though it could melt in the hot sun. Immediately upon entering the temple we were flooded with joy, as light greeted us from every corner and from the many open windows the sounds of birds reached our ears.

The temple gives a deepening, rounding quality to one who has earnestly pursued his night work and endeavored to live in balance on the path of Color. To the more recalcitrant, the temple offers a prodding, making him more aware of the things he has left undone and how he might better be living life on earth.

A floral decked winding staircase with a graceful curved design led us into the examination rooms. I was tested on lions of criticism and jealousy, and shown a greater need for tolerance and respect, while not expecting my own standards to be met by others. We were fed colors of the Arc of Spiritual Yellow as well as the opaline of the 10th color of Spiritual Blue, meaning spiritual balance, discerning between imagination and revelation of truth, integration of the spiritual powers of sight and hearing. This color helps us to interpret dreams and visions with deeper insight.

We're shown how Color will help us to have greater love and respect for all men, penetrating beyond the personality into the channel of our being. We testified to the fact that our earth lives have been changed very specifically through Color, that these subtle changes that have taken place in our actions and reactions have been made clear and definite to our minds.

In a room with a high dome narrowing at the top, much like the shape of the capitol dome, we gazed upward at gorgeous shades of yellow reflected on the crystal and glass pattern of the walls and ceiling. Silently, fully, we were fed until we contained as much light as we could encompass, and marveled at the interrelatedness of all things. We knew we had earned this privilege through our application and faithfulness, and that all can attain this who seek earnestly and live in accordance with balance and the law of love.

VIOLET There are ten golden steps which those seeking truth mount. The steps are not attained singly, being qualities of spirit which must become innate for attainment.

HELEN VON GEHR In the Temple of Enlightenment, just before my vision closed, there was this shower like sparklets. I thought they resembled waterless raindrops, but were more electrically charged than that, and they were all different colors.

RUBY I was aware of working on my lions of the Eightfold Path when I was impressed by the 5th psychological color of red, grayed olive green with the dirty orange midray, meaning greed. This color reveals a selfish, grasping nature with an intense desire for possessions, wealth and power. Greed is an offshoot of anger. I realize that the colors of generosity, the 11th of psychological green, and love, the 7th color of psychological red, will help modify the lion of greed, and soon, I was enveloped in those colors. I never thought of myself as a greedy person, but I was shown how insidious greed can be, how subtle, how it can hide and disguise itself, concealing itself from our discernment.

HELEN FLATWED I too was aware of a subtle lion that hides and can be hard to identify. I experienced the 1st psychological color of green: murky green with the clouded apricot midray, denoting indifference. This combination reveals insensitivity, disinterest and apathy. How easy it is to be indifferent! Indifference is the line of least resistance, ignoring responsibility, sinking into oblivion and self regard. It's a form of selfishness that we keep under wraps.

MIRIAM WILLIS The soft apricot in the midray without the cloudy gray overlay will help to overcome indifference.

LENORE It's amazing to me how our natures are being refined to a greater and greater degree. It's not that we're predominately indifferent in all situations, but that the quality pops up here and there in our lives until we acknowledge the failing and determine to be entirely rid of it. And that's what we experience when we encounter these lions along the way on the Eightfold Path.

****

THE TEMPLE OF POISE

MARY A visit to the Temple of Poise is not attained before one has climbed the steep way leading from the Temple of Enlightenment through seven tests. This temple, molded and unified with its promontory setting, is bathed in a constant glow of vibrant colors. It is a temple of promise that holds out to mankind good wishes interwoven with simplicity, orderliness, humility and truth. Foundations of faith support a superstructure of purest gold, with amber windows reflecting the rosy tints of dawn and dusk like gold Tiffany glass. As we wind slowly up a green sward and approach this apparition of loveliness, it seems our very heart aches in the desire for poise and beauty.

The temple in appearance is of crystalline loveliness, with pure crystal pillars and corridors of colored crystal. Its shape is like the letter "T" that beams aloft its identity, having the precept of truth and composure. It is beautiful in perfect balance, with clusters of corridors and structures which relieve its stark simplicity.

Our guides meet us in the courtyard and lead us through pathways to the inner chamber of contemplation. Here one is empowered to achieve a balance of mind, emotions, desires and spiritual expression in order to pass the tests of earth life with courage. Moderation in all things is not poise, but discipline. Poise is reacting in balance, dignity, courage and peace to the importunings of nature, self and others.

This then, is the setting for the masters who would speak and counsel with the living throng. To each and all they endow a cloak of peace whose warp and woof are made of fibers of strong balance. Strands of inner poise give protection from strife, the price we pay to reach this lofty peak.

This temple is located in a realm of incomparable beauty. As we walked down the broad avenue of trees and gardens, we formed part of a great concourse of people all proceeding in the same direction. Drawing close to the temple, we could feel ourselves being charged with spiritual energy, power supplied by the presence of teachers and messengers from the higher planes.

A very fitting place to receive the Father's representatives, this Temple of Poise. The building itself is sheer magnificence – stately, grand, like a great shaft of crystal, pure inspiration to behold. It is not transparent. Massive pillars are polished until they shine like the sun, while every carving flashes its brilliant colors until the whole edifice is a temple of light.

The sanctuary of spacious dimensions was filled with beings from the higher realms. The focus of attention was on the space in the center of the room where colors swirled. We saw before us a form. It is impossible to convey one fraction of the exaltation of spirit we felt in its presence. Many of us felt their spiritual life had just begun. With a final benediction upon us, this resplendent and truly regal being was gone from our sight.

Our teacher's subject was illumination through spiritual poise. The beauty and strength of this poise lies in its simplicity and in expression of certain truths which all men innately normally accept, the truth that behind all outer seeming is the great Creator God; the motivating power that both love and intelligence are effects of God's will; and finally, the self-evident truth that only through humanity can the divine plan be manifest.

A prayer was offered, a plan calling all mankind to the challenge of love in service, that an awakened mankind should bring forth God's intention that each soul become aware of its supremacy, enter the door of initiation, and simultaneously, the door into the world of spiritual reality should open to him. The divine purpose will then, through changed hearts and goals of humanity, be achieved.

The avenues to poise are the temple's corridors. They include courage, faith, endurance, equanimity, courtesy, humility, fortitude, bravery, and creative expression. These passageways are connected and lead to an enormous amphitheater with a heliotrope glow. I wonder where the stage is, and am told, "The stage is every individual present. Each of you is the stage on which these events are imprinted. Each of you presents his soul for balancing in the scales of life eternal. The lions on the path being met are cast into the arena, and the results of those encounters are writ upon your foreheads."

Each soul is introduced to experiences and challenges designed to awaken within the eternal elements of expansive love that is ever poised in a state of equilibrium, resting in the power of spiritual awareness.

A soul is silently ready for the unexpected yet expected; it is constantly prepared for all paradoxes. In perfect faith, it is ever on the alert, at peace with itself, perfectly aware of the call of spirit to go forward. It is in a state of tranquility, yet actively obedient. In deepest humility, it offers itself as a messenger for the divine call, tranquil no matter what the nature of that call to service involves. It is an exquisitely peaceful joy to be poised, for the poised soul is a dweller in both worlds, at home in either. Like a great shaft of crystal, it is in rapport with all that is human, yet filled with that which is more rarified and capable of fulfilling all earthly assignments as well as heavenly ones. And grace, its temple pure, is nothing less than peace with self, peace with mankind, and peace with the master mind. Bless you, all of you. Bless your earth lives.

MIRIAM WILLIS As one develops on the Path and extended vision is given, nature anoints one with the humblest as well as the grandest aspects of the Kingdom. We discern golden glints of truth within musty and antiquated myths. These shining facets free us from narrow, limited concepts, and every common bush becomes afire with God's love.

Poise is a state of being in equipoise, being so perfectly balanced that in one's life one reflects qualities of beauty, truth, love, and compassion that were displayed by the Master. It is a state much like the pendulum of a clock or the balance of the three bodies controlled by the power of spirit in perpetual motion, because of that power constantly flowing through the entire being, coordinated and poised. The same bands of color rayed out on the inside, focusing in the center into the white light of the Christ.

BILL Working with the Eightfold Path on the 8th Plane as we are, we're struck how far the world is from ideal. Every day we recognize how this planet expresses an unfortunately low level of consciousness – so much darkness, so many people in error, widespread selfishness and hatred. As spiritual seekers, we can't change the world, but we can change ourselves. And if enough people would embrace that idea, the world too, could change.

ANDREW There's time for development to happen, infinite time. Humanity will evolve in time.

DAN The Hindus have given us four long ages, called Yugas. Currently, we're living in the early stages of the Iron Age, the Kali Yuga, the age that's the lowest in consciousness, which began with the death of Krishna. Its first 5,000 years ended in 1898. We have 427,000 more years before the close of it. Following this present age, the world can look forward to the Bronze Age, followed by the Silver Age, and at last the Golden Age, when the world will be manifesting superior evolvement for at least two million years.

JOHN BASINSKI The life span for the entire universe, according to the ancient seers, is 314,159,000,000,000 solar years, or One Age of Brahma.

FRED So humanity has a long way yet to go.

****

THE TEMPLE OF KEYNOTE AND COLOR

MIRIAM WILLIS After leaving the Temple of Poise, our soul is filled with exultant joy, hope and faith, lifting us into a higher dimension of grace. Filled with this spirit, we journey on until we reach a point on the steep where we encounter a side road which is labeled the Temple of Keynote and Color.

This temple stands on a grand mesa, rising foursquare in vast dimensions. It has four pinnacles with a great dome in the center that gleams in the brilliant light of palest, delicate yellow-green shot through with azure blue. One is reminded of the 12th of green – at-one-ment with God, the height of growth in the Spiritual Arc of Green. The temple is reflected in all its beauty from a soft greyed pink lavender of harmony foundation to its crowning glory in the smooth still waters surrounding it. These reflections are so perfect that one instantly registers the realization "as above so below." The lights play about the fountains and flowers that we pass, as the path appears in a vision: love, light, color, service.

One glides over an arched bridge of developing power bordered by the royal purple of faith, and enters an outer chamber through a mother of pearl door framed in amethyst where one is met by his sponsor or guardian angel. Joy lights the mind and soul. One is led to a small chamber filled with his keynote color. Here he rests on a couch of faith and enters a deep stillness through which soft music in the cadences of his keynote interpenetrate his being. In this power, the first of his initiations are revealed and become stabilized according to the degree of his development. He feels absorbed into the peace that passeth all understanding, knowing that God's love will sustain him in the fulfilling of his destiny. This experience is one of ineffable love and joy. Hear the words, listen, trust and obey.

MARY   Why should we see our own aura and hear our keynote? It's a part of higher consciousness to be able to see our aura and hear our chord. When we're able to see and hear not only in our own sphere but in others, we have a light upon our pathway and we no longer walk in darkness. The regular use of our keynote tone and keynote color balances our three bodies and is a catalyst for harmonious relationships. We're always seeking harmony — in the world, in our families and everywhere. If we stop to check our thinking, we might find there's very little harmony within us a good amount of the time. So often we feel we have to get off to ourselves and into a perfect calm condition in order to sense harmony. But harmony is supposed to be a living force, an energy given to one to partake of spiritual principles. Harmony must be within first; then it will flow outward.

When we're in balance we're in harmony. We have to start appreciating the things we have before we can bring peace and harmony in the world. This is a truth that the teachers on the other side try to impress. Take the bitter with the sweet, and really work for a calming peace within.

Our aura gives us a clue to the states of mind that are active within and offers us an easy avenue through which we may pass into higher states of being. Every thought, spoken or unspoken, registers in the aura. Every feeling expressed or unexpressed registers. Our aura may become a cloud by day and a pillar of fire by night. It may be flung around us like a robe shedding light upon our soul's journey, or shutting us into the darkness of the damned.

Our keynote is ever with us in our place in the universal choir. Each of us has a voice in the music of the spheres, and whether we hear it or not, we take our place and sing our song. There are many whose song of life has been confused into a funeral dirge, when all around them is the master voice singing to call them back into harmony.

ESTHER BARNES Monday morning, I had a remembrance of this marvelous, triumphant singing of a large group of people, like a wave in the ocean, that power.

MIRIAM WILLIS In the vibration of singing, one of necessity must breathe more deeply, and in the upward growth of spiritual man, how we need to breathe in the rhythm of the holy breath. It's helpful to remember that singing comes from the very soul itself, therefore the vibratory rate of that which we sing would ring through our entire body, which has a marvelous uplifting quality. When we hum, let that humming go through the whole of your body; it's quite wonderful. I know you feel this when you sing your keynote. And then, the great Creator has given us not only our keynote, but our keynote color.

MARY We prove it with what we've brought through.

MIRIAM ALBPLANALP A chord of color, as a chord in music, sends overtones of powerful wavelengths of energy pouring into ever widening circles of influence. Just in such a ratio is the effect of one note, one chord, or one song by a symphony and choir in its degree of sonic and chromic blessing to man.

We homo sapiens are God's greatest instrument to vibrate to the universe's powerful energies of light, love and silent sound, an energy yet to be discovered. It is produced by the inner vibrating of spiritual consciousness and its circle of influence is to the ends of the universe. This is the electromagnetic sound-color we aurically answer in response to the song of love from above. It is the prime healing force of all, the therapy of therapies, the eternal blessing of ultimate, omnipotent peace, omni-dimensional and timeless. The instrument in joyous harmony with the music of the spheres, each sounding his keynote, each radiating concurrent color, each energizing spiritual atomic fission, is man raised to live his heritage. This is man as he is in minute number but can be in infinite magnitude, man raised to Christ Consciousness and living in the promised heaven on earth.

ESTHER BARNES On Wednesday morning I was aware of half opened delicately carved gates. They were made of what looked like ivory. They reminded me of the decorative artwork on the top of the Taj Mahal. Tonight in meditation I remembered the gates lead into the temple gardens.

VIOLET The temple is pillared loveliness in purest white atop a rise. Upon near approach one found that showing between the slender columns was color, and this color ran the scale of ivory to deep golden, followed by softest pink to a deep old rose. Walking completely around the temple, one found sections of blues and greens, shading from light to darker tones, at one end the purples and mauves, at the other, a wondrous shading of dove gray to violet and on into the colors of the rainbow. All this gave a gem-like effect of rare beauty, a scintillating aspect of richness in tone and texture.

This is a temple where everyone finds the color of their keynote. Surrounding the temple on all sides is clearest water making a reflecting pool from which one receives a double picture of line and color. Crossing over this pool are oriental like raised bridges, eleven in number, all symbolic of the power given by Christ to his disciples, and to us when we qualify.

GERTRUDE This temple stands for that delicate balance between the individual soul and its maker. Inside, each one follows the color of their own keynote, which carries one to the center of the pavilion where we all meet, where the sounding of all the keynotes creates music in glorious chords of sound. One absorbs the full power of the sound and color that pertains to them, and there is built into them the qualities that were less developed, needing implementation.

MIRIAM WILLIS Each of us is tested in stability, serenity, relaxation, patience, alertness and discipline. Each is aware he cannot fully pass these tests. The seeker also knows he must demonstrate through training received in these temples that he has been given a power to pursue love and its handmaidens: wisdom, balance, and peace, in order to manifest the true light and bring forth the illuminating energy from which God consciousness grows.

MARY Color is universal. This truth is found in old Sanskrit texts. Our Color Channel ties in with the spiritual aspirations of all men everywhere, as these are colors that express the universal clarity of spiritual desire and aspiration. When one's mind can sense the soothing rays of color, one knows he can accomplish the next climb on the Mount of Renunciation. We can't create a miracle, but we can be a part of it by holding the force of power in color for that miracle to happen.

The search of the soul after God and the finding of God is the supreme desire of everyone on the path of life. God, the universal consciousness, has set innumerable guideposts that point the way. We can read our records and our pathway in the stars; we can read them in our hand; we read them in our faces and in form, in the numbers of our name, in the very color of our hair and eyes and the tone of our voices. And yet, in the midst of all the wonderful signs that have stood forever between God and man, the greater part of humanity works on in disappointment and despair. "The light shineth in the darkness, but the darkness comprehendeth it not."

The seeker knows the pathway to consciousness of God is through human consciousness, and only as he knows himself can he know the universal secrets. "They shall be taught of God," Jesus said. Man does not go far in his search before he finds that we are all named, numbered, colored, and faced in a perfect universal and personal plan.

The Path leads the seeker to truth no matter where he wanders. Then finding himself, he naturally seeks to relate this self with things around him. As the search continues, he pushes out into a world of activity so great that he's bound to pause to master one thing at a time, and through this mastery, unlock the door to the next chamber of experience. In the beginning of the search for knowledge, as man comes to a world of color and sound, he turns in rightful questioning to gain the mysteries of these things. The world of Color is so wonderful that it bewitches his senses, and then as he extends his vision into deeper inclusion, he finds a world of sound that enters his senses jars him into further mystery. Turning then to this world of color and sound around him, he asks at first blindly, where am I? What is this? And the Universal Mind of which he is a part must answer.

And it does answer, by giving him comprehension until he can ask and answer his own seemingly unanswerable questions. It has been written, "Ask and ye shall receive. Seek, and ye shall find." And after one has sought, found and known the reason of the seeking and finding, he is comforted with the joy of his understanding. When one has opened his vision to the color scheme of the universe and his ears to the wonderful harmony around, he knows that higher seeing and hearing bring added power and peace. In finding the law of his own aura and his keynote, he can ring true as a strong instrument and shine as a lamp unto the feet of the uninitiated.

The universal life strips one thing after another off the personal until one stands bared to the center and sees the true reflection of the self. When daily we can increase the light of the universal, we grow naturally into at-one-ment with vibrant levels of divine light. Our eyes are not blinded with celestial glare, but are strong enough to look into the very highest creative law of life.

No man can escape himself; no man can escape his responsibility to himself to release that which is within his plan of life, namely, an unfolding expression of the blueprint he came into this life with. As the wheel of life turns, tests become more severe, but as our understanding grows, our tests are welcome and joyful experiences. Only when the soul is awakened can we understand what is given in the higher light. We're seeking soul illumination so that all our outward expressions shall be as perfect as our true selves.

Color is a measure of true spirituality. The Color Channel brings balance in thinking, patience in waiting for belief to develop into faith's unique security. The seeker knows life's pattern as traced upon his soul at birth will be given to him again through dreams, visions and the revelations received in night work in the halls of memory and in the temples of learning. Development in spiritual power through the Color Channel is an intuitive gift that causes one to burst forth in the rapture of faith and to listen for the whispers of love and the promise of eternal life.

Remember, illumination comes from within. When the heavier colors in our aura are transmuted into positive ones, we live in a state of not just believing: we know.

******

THE TEMPLE OF SILENCE

MIRIAM WILLIS It is with new buoyancy and grace that one journeys forth from the Temple of Keynote and Color to the steep toward the Temple of Silence. Examine within your expanded consciousness for fresh meanings in the tests we face on the stations as we climb: tolerance, devotion, peace, constancy, fortitude, selflessness, gratitude. As one draws nearer, walking in a deep, cool and shaded forest of trees, a mysterious atmosphere of stillness of nature seems to scarcely breathe, lest the spell be broken. We see a shaft of sunlight ahead as we leave the Forest of Unknowing to enter a garden of fragrant flowers and herbs. This fragrance is spicy and elusive. All is clothed in modest beauty where one must hunt through the foliage for half hidden blossoms.

Stillness continues to pervade the hush of evening. The peace that fills the scene is almost tangible and very sustaining, and now there is a glow of moonlight which casts silvery haze over all. Our eyes behold a lovely temple in the center of a clear blue lake, reflecting its shining colors from the purples of its foundation through pink lavenders of inspiration, opaline blue of spiritual balance, and the azure blue of fourth dimensional reality.

We crossed the lake over the bridge of spiritual balance, a suspension bridge which was easy to travel when one stepped out in rhythm and in balance of all the senses. A teacher met us and we followed a lighted path to a doorway with the all-seeing eye above it. We went into a central room in which light was rayed down upon us in a cone shape from jewel like openings in the dome above.

The temple is modest, elusive and beautiful, like a moonstone in substance and color. One enters through a narrow door and is astonished at the brilliance and glorious color within. It is as though this center of light that at first almost blinds is the cause of the restrained reflection without. We seem to merge with it in a synthesis of rapport and with an inflow of understanding.

So filled with light is this profound silence, not a word is spoken, not a sound heard, yet one is filled with rapture that embraces all one's companions in unison of spirit and joy. One realizes the need to come to this hallowed temple many times to develop the power of sustaining silence within the soul, until through practice one can enter a clear field of quietude where his mind is indeed stilled, his spiritual ears attuned, and his consciousness lifted to the reality of the oneness of two worlds.

The beauty and strength of this temple lie in its simplicity and in the central truths which all men innately accept.

MARY Would you enter into this realm of happiness? Would you wish to tell another seeker of the glories of the temples of heaven? We need to realize that not our physical but our spiritual nature is the dominant part of us. It is the monarch that holds sway over the rest of us. Live with patience and in faith go forth into the silence as an alchemist distilling precious sweetness from life's sorrows. And then from Sanskrit: "The desert of desire in every life is crossed by experiencing God's love."

LOUISE It was night, and I was in a deep forest of towering trees. I had no idea where I was, but I was unafraid. As I walked forward, I came to a clearing filled with light. I saw clouds of beautiful colors. When they broke, I saw a castle whose spires rose until they were out of sight. I simply stood, awestruck, and looked.

I was not invited in, but nevertheless, I was filled with joy and peace, content to be where I was.

MARY I'd say it was a good omen to start with, having been given a glimpse into the other world and having seen a temple. That's usually the welcome; they come quickly, they go quickly, and you doubt, almost, you're seeing them, but it's a good start. That's what we build our foundations of faith upon.

We're in the magnificent Temple of Silence. One voice is heard, the voice of our Lord. We all know it's he who's speaking and to us – it seems individually – because the warmth of our need and our response is as if we were tied hand in hand with him, yet we may be with a multitude of people. And that's the power of that great individual; that's what he has said: "Where I am, there shall ye be also." His voice, clear as a bell and vibrant with truth, rings out over the vast throng of people who listen in a hush of great awe. He tells us the miracle of healing the broken happens whenever through faith, the energies of divine life are liberated.

I feel we have touched the hem of his garment when we've heard him speak -- the ringing voice, the magnificent personality that comes through. I've not seen the Christ face; I've only seen a great figure standing clothed in beautiful color. And if I ever do see his face, I don't believe I'd have eyes to see him, because the spectacle is enough; it's all I can contain as it is. And each of you, as you heard the Voice, said to me, one by one, "Oh, if we could only carry those ringing tones within our very soul; if only we could realize that he is ever with us."

Then one of you said, "My mother used to talk about his everlasting arms." Those everlasting arms are there waiting for us. I believe he is as a mother/father spirit to us, that he receives us in that way, and that's why we feel we're his own. I'm not talking emotionally, I'm talking out of a language of the Kingdom of the Christ. I know the doubts and the fears I've lived through, I also know what it is to overcome, what it is to suffer and to suffer with each one of you when you go through times of worry. You're always so welcome in my heart. God bless each one of you.

LOLA This is the right wing of the Temple of Silence: As you travel the Path you're guided, although you're not always conscious of that guidance. At times a solution appears as your need is expressed, either audibly or silently in the yearning of the soul.

One of the greatest desires of the seeker is for greater vision, which has led you to this place on the upward journey. You emerge from the dense forest into a clearing where the light is dazzling, and when you've become accustomed to this, you pass through an alpine meadow with beautiful flowers, lush grass, trees that seem to bend to greet you in a gentle, fresh clear atmosphere. Your soul is attuned; your sense of expectation leads you on.

We began to see inwardly. Our character revealed to us dispositional traits highlighted for our special attention when we would return to earth. Then a great light began to form in the room, reaching its outermost walls, and the Voice spoke: "When you've practiced seeing in others what I see in them, you shall begin to have the spiritual vision you desire. Developing the third eye is possible for all. Be aware, love thy neighbor as thyself. Peace be unto you."

VIOLET We walked over a carpet of an infinite variety of flowers in all imaginable shades. It was soft and comforting underfoot. So intent were we in admiring the flowers that suddenly, looking up, there stood the temple. It had strong and beautiful lines within and without. We were completely bathed in silence, as in the hush of twilight or early dawn, when the earth is veiled in mystery. There was about this temple that same serene majesty where one felt close to God's presence.

One was conscious of unlimited power, the supremacy of all the good, and one felt the inner meaning of Christ's presence. Realizing all this, there crept into conscious conception the innate possibilities divinely implanted within each soul. Then the focus turned upon one's own soul and upon all that soul could demonstrate in life on earth. A lecture helped each seeker evaluate his present development with a vision opening into future spiritual sensing, growing in knowledge of the colors needed for this awareness. This was given as a silent prayer.

ANDREW The people we see at night from other groups, are they too on the Eightfold Path as we are?

MARY Many of them are. There's a place for all in the Kingdom. I find that so many people from other teachings we encounter in our night adventures have great wisdom. And through the silence, they receive as much as we do. In the temple along with us this week were people of all nations. We walked with the multitude, a vast throng through that temple; everyone was enlightened and moved through in meditation. There was the one voice and the feeling within ourselves that we were the only individuals there. For a moment, we touched that split between ourselves and our souls, and felt we would never leave there. It was just a touch; and so it says to go through meditation. Meditation is the control of emotions, and most of all it is the control of the mind that one needs.

JEANNE I sat by a rocky shore in the brilliant sun, surrounded by water, talking to people from many walks of life. The water was rough, and I felt I was on an island. Above, the sky was filled with cumulus clouds, and the color was a strong cobalt blue, the 4th color of spiritual blue. Gray overtones provide the holding force of a great, usable power to control emotion and to prevent waste of power.

In speaking with a teacher, areas were revealed to me where I had blocked out light and truth. I was filled with feelings of universality and awareness of God working in all lives, no matter at what stage of development the person, no matter what path he walks. This was a needed lesson for me, inasmuch as I had become snobbish about our path.

In the distance, upon the summit of a hill, I saw the temple, surrounded with a grayish mist like a veiling over it. Through the mist appeared a grey lavender structure, square in shape, with other appendages or wings. Inside the veil, the material was lush and alive. To my vision it looked as if many paths led to the temple, and I was told that visible to my eyes were eighteen paths taken by earth initiates, all seeking knowledge into the mystery of the human mind, such knowledge as is revealed step by step in the temples of vision along the planes.

In order to arrive at the temple, it was necessary to find one's way though a golden labyrinth. I was told many become lost and confused in this maze, but for one who has faithfully followed the path of development in this teaching, endeavoring to follow guidance, stay in balance and live the inner teachings, it is natural.

After the labyrinth, we climbed up many golden steps at a short angle, proceeding across a moat. The sky was clear now, the atmosphere no longer misty. The veil over the temple had lifted and the gates swung wide.

I found myself in a very large temple with a central courtyard, rooms to the sides of it, each one containing a different group at worship or in class. The ground of the central part was of beige stone. I visited at least seven of the rooms. I was led into a place with a vermillion atmosphere like flames. I walked through and came to a room where a blonde wooden chest stood containing records I was to look at, revealing some of my past attitudes.

Then I went through a test, which seemed easier than many of the previous tests I've had in my night work, because this time I was given a cloak to wear that made me feel invulnerable and unassailable. After this test, I was told the cloak was like color, that if I had the faith, color could be just as miraculous. Next I was led to a table where several people sat, including Mary. I had the feeling that they had been waiting a long time for me to arrive in their midst, at this particular point along the path. They invited me to sit down.

At the end of the night, I walked over gray cobblestones, seeing another large group of people coming toward me, perhaps a group from another part of the world ready to commence their night work. I was wearing white, purified after the night of testing and learning.

MARY That's the Temple of Silence, the West wing.

MARGARET In the Temple of Silence, the light is unto the soul as much as he can encompass; the paths are lit by one's own faith. There's a place called the Cloister. It seemed to me that here there were hints of things to come, and that what was dimly seen was dim because it was perceived only slightly in the consciousness.

In this temple there are great areas of stillness and perfect beauty. Here one hears the song of his own soul as its deflections and challenges are met. One's thoughts react only to oneself. Absolute avoidance of vocal participation is a must in this high, rarified vibration. Out of the silence comes the ethereal dawn of new conscious awakening to the spirit within. Silence encircles one with its greatness. It's a stillness one feels here, creation about to burst forth from the human soul. The silence dwells in consciousness and grows. The silence deepens, widens, and gives all that is within a chance to be magnified to the end that anything discordant may be disintegrated to its elements and recast. Color, tended by masters, sweeps through. One does nothing but worship in his heart and offer all to the Creator.

Out of the silence comes the music of all creation. To be co-creator with God, one needs be pure of purpose, pure in heart and willing to do one's highest bidding. This is a temple of purification and magnification. At one time I was aware of the colors of royal purple and silver. Twice this week I was shown vividly what I took to be banners of orders of service, I believe the Order of the Fifteen. One was a thick looking turquoise cross ornamented with gold against a purple background, and the other was a banner, five-sided, of red lilac crisscrossed with gold cords. This had a border of the color of divine imagination around it, the 4th color of the Spiritual Arc of Purple, rose-purple amethyst, the open door to higher consciousness. And right against the banner was a pair of men's white dress gloves.

DAN   Margaret mentioned "orders of service" and "the Order of the Fifteen." I don't understand what that is.

MARY   The Order of the Fifteen is one of the orders one earns through development on the Planes. You begin to bring back experiences of your night work and life on the inner planes. You're chosen for certain Orders, and those will have an influence on what you do when you go to the other side of life to live after your transition. So it's a course of training, a course of purification and one of realization of who you are, then to build within yourself a self respect through self knowledge.

DAN   About meditation: to what extent does it enter into our relationship with the Temple of Silence?

MARY The relationship is this: one never goes to the Temple of Silence unless they've learned meditation in some form. Remember that there are many faiths with different forms of meditation in the temple, people of all nations, and we walk with the multitude, a vast throng – there's a place for all in the Kingdom. At the same time, we have the feeling within ourselves that we are the only individual there. Just for the moment when we touched that spot between ourselves and our soul, we felt truly enlightened.

In the Temple of Silence, we're of one mind in the light. Although there are many faiths and practices in the temple, everyone hears in his own tongue. It's the great Voice, and it's the one voice you never forget. You hear it first in the Temple of Bells — a bell-like voice. We take it back with us, never forgetting the words which we keep like a motto to live by. We don't see God. We just know there's a great creative force that fashioned this world and stands above all other things, because all teachers and Christ point to the Father, the great Creator.

****

CHAPTER 8

THE TEMPLE OF VISION

As the seeker travels along the steeps of further progression from the Temple of Silence, he begins to realize more fully that positive fullness of the building qualities he received there. His tests are deeply searching, and he is grateful for added strength. These tests reveal a greater need in life for tolerance, love, patience, constancy, fortitude, selflessness and gratitude. As he passes each test he goes back one station to help a brother, and together they progress to the next station. He discovers he can't advance without silently sharing the power he has gained with another.

MIRIAM WILLIS Here is Mary's gift to us for tonight, from the Temple of Vision:

"As in group formation we walk toward the Temple of Vision, our eyes behold a cloud. To me, it was of a green tint streaked with spirals of amber rose and capped with a canopy of blue. This cloud was continuously in motion, and at length grew into the shape of a stately pavilion whose roof was of deepest blue violet with pillars of amber rose and purple. There were in all eight pillars at the side and back, also two on either side of the main opening in front. These latter two were deep violet with spiraled bands of crimson edged with white.

"All were pulsating with the light of those who were entering this gem of beauty. From the pavilion came a soft murmur of melody most wonderful to feel. The brilliance and transparency was as a golden amber mist. The atmosphere cleared, and before us we beheld a golden altar banded in ruby colored gems. A teacher led us forward to our seats, where many great ones of the heaven world waited to give instruction to those who were ready to receive their message.

"The teacher's message was the most vital I have thus far heard. Some will remember these words: 'Give your message without thought of how it may be received.' Because of certain things he said, I recognized John, the beloved disciple of Jesus. 'As people seek to evolve spiritually,' he said, 'they recognize the soul's call to come into the heritage of development. They answer that call by lifting their eyes from the dust and seek to read from the pattern of their life what is next on the path of development. It is your task to help mankind in spiritual unfoldment, you who have found God through love and years of service.'"

GLENN As a class, we approached the temple together with many others who came from all directions and different walks of life, races and creeds. Here the river of life was quickened into abundant availability. One's eyes and ears expanded in keenness of perception and receptivity. We were enveloped in a golden haze. Presently, the Temple of Vision appeared as a central focal point of power drawing this great conclave of people irresistibly through the golden haze. It was most glorious to behold, with foundations of deep blue violet marble shot through with fuchsia and orchid, becoming more delicate in hue and tint as it rose toward the sky.

One seemed to pass through a door of divine imagination and walk down a corridor of the same rich color. This gave one both light and penetrating power that led to a great chamber. Here we found a vast, curved substance that was moving but seemed like a screen of divine imagination, rose-purple amethyst, the open door to higher consciousness. On the floor in front of it was a large mirror. The surrounding area was filled with moving, exquisitely beautiful multicolored rays too numerous to name that contributed a supporting quality flowing through each one of us and focusing on the great curved screen accompanied by soft, ethereal music. This was interpreted as the sound vibrations of the colors.

We stood silently listening and looking expectantly at the screen. As our concentration deepened, picture after picture appeared in symbols that we interpreted according to our understanding and degree of development. Each picture was clearly reflected in the mirrored substance in such a way that we realized heavenly visions were meant to be applied in the earth life for further growth in development. Our whole being expanded in wondrous awe at the lavish abundance of the great Creator's provision.

As we left the temple with others of all races and religious predilections, an enormous surge of love caused us to realize the brotherhood of man, and with our heavenly guides and teachers, we burst into a paean of praise and thanksgiving, We were conscious of angels in a higher strata near us singing the most glorious descant in bell like overtones.

LINDA What is the definition of vision?

MIRIAM WILLIS   Vision is something supposedly seen by other than normal sight; something perceived in a dream or trance, or supernaturally revealed as to a prophet; the ability to perceive something not actually visible through mental acuteness or keen foresight. One also speaks of a force or power of imagination, mental or spiritual.

One learns to distinguish between psychological imagery and spiritual imagery. Our ability to close our eyes and journey in imagination to far places is a gift. Fantasy and daydreaming are forms of imagination. These lie in the realm of psychological imagery. The ability to create mental pictures is related to the ability to receive visual impressions from the higher realms, to have visions and to recall dreams.

LINDA   And vision is a part of development, applied to the spiritual journey?

MARY To go forward on the path of development, we must have the vision to think we're not as we see ourselves, but as God sees us. And the sum total of ourselves must be realized, which means self respect and "know thyself," to know the worthiness and the height of that soul, the length and the depth of where it can take you. So to "know thyself," we have to know the God within, that God within who readily speaks to help us. With those words in mind, let's think what we heard this day or last night that we can give forth. Has there been a proof within your mind that God does listen? That you've been spoken to? That the small voice of conscience has corrected you? That you've been led in some mysterious way to do something you didn't intend to do? That you've dared to do the thing you hesitated to do because you feared the results?

Doesn't fear inhibit us, preventing us from doing so many things? Can we not trade that fear for an element of faith, and on that faith, place ourselves, our personalities, most of all our egos that command our respect every day. So let us think we can forget ourselves in remembering the soul of ourselves, that we can forget our likes or dislikes, and instead desire to know more of the reality of ourselves. Ask yourself, do I believe, or am I just feigning a belief? Do I want to walk through dead leaves of yesterday or under the green tree just coming into bud? The path is there, either way we take it, and we need to have the courage to step higher, to break into a new road of life. Have you thought I alone choose, or do you have the faith to say, "I and the Father are one"?

The world has ever been the same through the evolution of mankind, but the more man evolves in his spiritual life, the more closely comes the day of enlightenment. "And I will come again and receive you unto myself. And where I am there shall ye be also." I have faith in those words we heard the great John speak in the temple. Many of you were there, and many of you heard those words. Take them to your heart and know. If you forgot to bring them through, it was because of a mind that was not quite attuned to the height where you were. God is not a selector of people. He created us all in his image, and we all have the same rights. But the man who has eyes and will not see will not have a vision.

MARGARET   There were pithy sentences accompanying the lessons in the Temple of Vision. We learned of the infinite vision of creation, the intricacies of love, the vitalizing forces that play upon our spirit when we're amenable to their influences and the sparking of life itself. Vision is the sparking of life energy at the same moment when the soul is ready to perceive. When one catches the rhythm of his own soul, he's able to harmonize with God's plan with ease. Vision is the harpsichord of life. The life plan is one of vision, vision to dare, to do, to hope, to believe, to affirm and have faith.

I asked why there's no verb for faith, and was told the nearest one is to know, and that faith is a substance. Sometimes we have to let it be in our consciousness somewhere, then it sneaks out of us.

MARY That's this week's temple, Temple of Vision.

VIOLET   The Temple of Vision, North Wing: Over all a pall of smoke was a greyness we had to penetrate. Then suddenly—light! This light seemed to come from everywhere. What glory! The color of everything was gold, as though a gossamer web covered it. When our eyes became accustomed to the brightness, there stood a temple. It looked as though made of purest gold shimmering in the light. There seemed individuality to this temple in some inexplicable way.

Hoping for answers, we entered this edifice. Inside, when our eyes became accustomed to the brightness, we perceived a long aisle and seats on either side. At the very end was an altar with many lights upon it. A magnificent pipe organ with far more keyboards, pipes and pedals than any earth organ was peeling forth in glorious tones whose sounds reached us in waves. A service was about to begin.

We seated ourselves in a group on the left hand side. Beauty and reverence were the atmosphere of this piece, and instinctively we prayed. The organ music continued with a changed tempo, as we all rose and there entered a choir of many voices of men, women, and boys vested. The robes they wore were of all different shades of color, all blending.

This procession had entered from the right, about half way up the nave. Now each member of the procession took their places in a special section just below the raised area on which the altar stood. An antiphonal now began, the choir singing, then the congregation, to organ accompaniment, a most inspiring act of praise. We instinctively seemed to know what to sing, and so could join in.

There entered a magnificent figure who shed light from his person who spoke to the people. His subject was on God's greatness in conception and manifestation, giving us illustrations from history, then taking us into the outreach of plan and design in the cosmic order. We learned much and were inspired. More beautiful music ensued; then this phase was over and we filed out.

As we left through the doorways, a guide spoke to each one of us and asked questions which elucidated answers whether we had understood the lesson given. This was done in the gentlest manner, in a love so pure that it could neither hurt nor discourage, only increase more deeply our desire to become one with our vision.

MARGARET Violet's description of the heavenly organ reminds me of something wonderful that happened this week in my earth life. I was given the rare privilege and great blessing of being allowed to play a very special organ. This organ has 17 ranks of different sounding musical instruments – flutes, reeds, strings – plus numerous percussion instruments – xylophone, marimba, chimes, bells, drums, cymbals, and so forth. It's a remarkable organ, a Wurlitzer. I'd never played anything like it, not on earth – only in heaven! And I must say, that as incredible as this organ is, it pales in comparison to the heavenly organs.

MIRIAM ALBPLANALP Mary, when people see things and remember visually, you can tell them where they're at and what's going on, but how do you explain the things that I get that are always in words? Do we hear those things? Or is that just bringing back a feeling, a sensing?

MARY No. You painted a picture. Your word picture was given me.

LOLA I was given a picture in which all the "rights" of the Eightfold Path were depicted in beautiful letters: right view, right aspiration, right speech, right action, right livelihood, right effort, right mindfulness, and right concentration. The understanding of what's needed to fulfill these spiritual goals in my life was firmly set in my consciousness. It was both an edifying and enlightening experience, and, I daresay, a beautiful vision.

PATTI I had a vision of a woman sitting on a bench. The only thing I can remember about her is that her dress was brilliant rose-blue heliotrope, if there is such a color. A small girl came and sat down beside her. Her dress was purest white. Now because I can't remember anything about them except the age of the people and their color, was this possibly a color treatment?

MARY No. The woman was of the physical, concerned with you, and the child was spiritual. I would say the woman was you, and the child was your spiritual being. The spiritual was all in white, and physical, you have used lots of color.

PATTI Why would one receive that, Mary?

MARY To show that we have a spiritual self, and the growth. We're all children in spirit, because we're living in the physical. We may have many lives behind us, but we're working on this life right here and now. Our past lives mean nothing until we redeem ourselves for why we came to the world this time. I don't talk on past lives. I think it would make it more interesting for you if I did. But you were sent here with a pattern to fulfill, and until I see that pattern etched in the very life of you, I would not feel I had a right to go back into past lives and tell you something of your back life. Understand?

ANDREW I got a message today that the color of spiritual alignment was known to the highest self, a kind of a pale blue like a holding force blue, only clearer and with a silvery overtone to it. Does that make sense?

MARY Yes. That's Christ's life.

ANDREW Silvery blue ...

MARY Yes, and your own soul.

******

THE TEMPLE OF WISDOM

MIRIAM WILLIS As we progressed up the steep from the Temple of Vision toward the Temple of Wisdom, we discovered the experience and growth we've thus far gained has awakened a searching hunger for greater depth and a better understanding of our visions and symbology.

The tests on the steeps show how we operate the power of God in our daily living and how love and wisdom enter our work. Our decisions may be moral, physical, psychical, elemental, cultural, sociological, financial, biological, filial, according to the developmental needs of the seeker.

Our approach to the great 8th Plane Temple of Wisdom is through a labyrinth of sorting out the true from the false, a learning to look past the outer into the heart of things. Each seeker is tested on seven stations in: sensing, perception, interpretation, hearing, humility, trust, and obedience.

Any lack or failure is highlighted, and we know that whatever stands in our way on the path to the Temple of Wisdom is ours to overcome. We are then empowered to see our way clear for the climb.

ANDREW   We've been to this temple before ... but on lower planes, not on the 8th Plane.

MIRIAM WILLIS   There are Temples of Wisdom on many planes, and we've been to several of them. We go to a Temple of Wisdom on increasingly higher planes. And this 8th Plane temple is a most fascinating place. There's an amazing flood of light in a rainbow which one must ascend and tread. As we go along this path, we come to the edge of a chasm where we find that the temple can be reached only by a rainbow bridge that spans a void of seeming nothingness requiring courage, poise and faith to venture forth. Some fail the test of faith and must climb up again. A seeker who responds to his soul urge floats with easy swiftness over the chasm, filled with as much divine love as it's able to receive.

The soul then returns to a pear shaped center, ascends in vibration to the narrower, higher neck, and is borne into the Temple of Wisdom from the right side, entering the reception court where, kneeling, one receives a particular initiation which is an eternal gain that is built into the aura.

JOHN BRANCHFLOWER   We come through a great lofty cathedral in the shape of a cross. Souls from the 8th and higher planes come here for initiations pertaining to wisdom and divine love. On such occasions one is taken by a high guide through the apse and down the nave to the crossing.

BERNARD   The temple is like a huge spider web of iridescent light reflecting all colors yet containing none, for it seems to be of pure spirit that reflects back to man his need as he projects such color or colors. This spider web structure has many different levels, and each person enters at the level of his development, the lowest level being the outer circumference ascending to the cross, which is the heart of divinity. It seems as though our fiercest lions of the Path were collected at this point for a going over. Any lack or failure or weak spot is highlighted by the tests – justice, mercy, courage, sorrow, emotional balance, sympathy.

LOLA   In the center is a raised dais with seats in circular formation for the hierarchy who guide and teach there. From this dais one can look out at all the wisdom of the ages, for the wisdom of every race and tribe is the substance that forms this spider web surrounding the central temple. At the center, eventually all things are understood and the soul is filled with divine wisdom.

One turns to the right across to the end, returning on the left. One's life and special aspects of it are lifted at the end, and soul value is revealed as one returns along the left side. This is done many times for self realization and understanding of divine wisdom.

The counsel given is, "Think over the loving care you have had in your life, the development, the causes for happiness."

He is then taken to the center of the crossing to a beautiful chapel of mother of pearl. This is as the womb of the soul's incarnation, and here the life of Christ is revealed with as much depth as the soul has the capacity of receiving. One passes through this so our souls will know an inner blossoming whose fruit will come into the light if we let it, for wisdom finds its way into the humble heart. We pass beneath triumphal arches domed high above in iridescent mother of pearl, a translucent aura through which moon and stars are seen. The air is soft and mellow, richly perfumed with delicate fragrance.

The great Voice speaks to us; the truth of its message vibrates in our hearts and remains there, ready for use in time of need. Such is the economy of God, however long this may take, for wisdom opens the very gates of heaven. Wisdom is the source and supply to man's crying need for brotherhood and unity, for wisdom is love divinely directed.

MARGARET   We approach by the Gateway of Humility and pass through the Court of Grace to this temple of magnificent grandeur which appears in glowing peach tones with fuchsia darts of light and sparkling jewels. The heights of the temple are out of sight. The temple covers a tremendous area and contains any number of labyrinthine passageways of varying colors where specialized wisdom is attained.

As we step inside, we see the floor is an apricot color shot with gold with gold lights. Here are many "pockets of wisdom," niches and cubbyholes to be discovered. The teaching is both general and personal. It included these words: "Favored is he who has won the right to be called wise, for wisdom is knowing God in his manifest forms and using that wisdom rightfully. Wisdom enhances and makes all gifts of the spirit, for these gifts are further empowered as one uses them wisely."

Wisdom empowers grace and helps it grow. Wisdom "back feeds" all the gifts, the keys and the qualities. Wisdom is an action. Think of it as right action in thought, words and in motion, fitting to the highest purpose of the moment, the glowing peach of union of mind and spirit making possible the expression of our highest wisdom potential. Wisdom of the sages and of the ages must be reinterpreted for today's needs. Therefore, go into the closet in your cloak of contemplation, and seek the presence of the Lord.

Wise use of vision begets more vision, more sensing, more knowing, and the total instrument becomes greater attuned for God's purpose. Wisdom nurtures all gifts of spirit. We were awed by the decorum of the wise witnesses to God's glory. I was told my purpose in life, which seems logical, after all the time spent last week on the life plan in the Temple of Vision.

HELEN MARSH The Temple of Wisdom is suspended this way: when you're looking up the hill, you can't see where there's anything that contains people. Yet every labyrinth, every alley, everything that's a corridor is a place where people are receiving paths to wisdom. And that's one of the things I remembered. I also remember that so many spots have taken on the color of buttercup yellow.

GEORGE FLOURNOY I was aware of increased life energy. And I saw several small spider webs. If you try to push them, you find there's a mirror behind them in which you see yourself, everything about yourself. And in a flash, you've been given so much understanding.

MARY I think probably that you were given a certain sense of balance, and the center was the antenna that reaches to God.

JEANNE I stood across a body of water observing the distant shore. Rays of the sun reflected on the misty water in colors of the 4th of Spiritual Yellow and the 10th of Spiritual Blue. The fragrance of aromatic pines filled my nostrils. It was on this path I met a test of fear. Following this I found myself in a mute forest of birch trees. All was silence but for the sounds of nature and a faint symphony of softly blended keynotes.

I was flooded with the royal purple faith, the 2nd color of the Spiritual Arc of Purple, as the desire for greater truth impelled me forward. Inside the temple, I was at first attracted to the many brightly colored tapestries in peacock, rose and turquoise, but felt the need to reach a higher dimension to find more refined colors. I approached a pale peach door with a golden aura surrounding it. A marble staircase led me to an examination room, where I was measured on my growth into greater perspective and was given insight and instruction on how to read the human psyche more accurately.

BARBARA Tuesday night, as the class was watching people of all nations march through the Temple of Wisdom, before me loomed a crowd of people dressed in the predominant color of rose. The people gave out such power. And as I listened, they were singing a beautiful chorus of praise to God.

MARGARET We ascended the steps, pausing on each rise to ponder our virtues and to search our own worthiness to appear before the hierarchy, who would meet us and ennoble us by their presence.

GLENN This was given in the Temple of Wisdom: Love is immortal. It buds on earth and blossoms through eternity. Love opens up broad avenues through which spirit may pass to higher and broader conceptions of life and bask in the sunlight of truth of which the undeveloped mind knows little. Love quickens and inspires the mind. It exalts, softens, and glorifies the entire being. Its mystic charm transforms cold, commonplace life; it adorns earth with the glory of heaven while its object takes on the highest attributes of the ideal.

Love is a benediction, a baptism from the highest, purest realm of life, thanksgiving, and prayer. Love and righteousness in balanced form are necessary for the purity that brings in the kingdom of the soul. The quality of love is intrinsic to all life. Love is the great invisible pattern of God's creation, the never ending answer to all the question marks in man's consciousness from the simplest to the most profound. Love, the 7th color of psychological red, is seen as pink rose lightly underlaid with pale orange.

SYLVIA As taught in the Temple of Wisdom: at-one-ment with the spiritual realm produces power. It's a process that creates life, energy, force, motion, propulsion and changes transformation of form, substance, quality, kind. One always needs more light to penetrate the darkened and shrouded recesses of memory consciousness, until the full light of truth illumines into clear reality. Then we know that its clarity and purifying ray will remove the cause of error and the mistakes of blindness, as a cataract removed from the human eye restores sight.

The only enemy is one's own bad disposition, habits of thought and opinion. When these are mastered, one becomes free. Look to the kingdom of the soul! Wisdom is the spirit and the atmosphere in which one abides; the thought of life, the motive power for development, and the unselfish end toward which one grows. Our goal is right view, right effort, right action.

MIRIAM ALBPLANALP Heard in the Temple of Wisdom, the angel of light speaks: "Why are your eyes not turned heavenward? Why do you look for answers amidst the ashes of your burned out hopes? Light is from above, not found on earth. Nor again is the answer written in men's blood or the sins of selfishness; it is written in glory in the heavens, in the light which grows in hearts of love and humility. For those hearts have found the pearl of great price, reflecting, generating the light of the eternal. Look up, beyond with fearlessness and hope: for all radiance of a plan lies written there for all opened eyes to read, and having read, to align themselves in confidence." Thus speaks the angel of light in love.

"Love can open the doors of beauty and of light. Clear the sight, make glad the heart. This is the miracle in which you increasingly play a part, which will blossom as love's store grows into riches of immensity and wisdom." This was received from our high guide Marcus, Teacher in the Temple of Wisdom.

MARGARET In assessing my experiences in the Temple of Wisdom, tying it to the lions and to the Rays of the Eightfold Path, I was struck how much the 4th Ray of the Eightfold Path, the Ray of Devotion, pertained to my goals. To be able to attain the truth of this ray, the Path as adventure and raising my consciousness into the permanent physical atom that opens into Cosmic Consciousness, I asked myself what is the most important lion that I must overcome? The answer is selfishness. So this is what I have been working on, through various different plumes, and with emphasis on my keynote of coral red, clear thinking and pure purpose, the 6th color of the Spiritual Arc of Red.

JOHN BASINSKI Right action is an important part of the Eightfold Path. I've been thinking of a great deal this week, for as Margaret said, wisdom is right action.

****

CHAPTER 9

THE TEMPLE OF POWER

MIRIAM WILLIS   After the experience in the Temple of Wisdom, it would seem that the soul had received all it could possibly contain. Yet there's within this consciousness a realization of power needed to operate an integration of forces, thus the urge to attain leads the soul to pursue its onward way.

Again man is tested through seven stations and given the opportunity to discover and develop enabling powers. Through this cleansing and developing process, the seven spiritual centers of being are enlivened and nurtured. In our night work, we actually see the operation of the vortex of these centers with their concentric circles extending farther with greater intensity. Such an experience deepens awe for the Creator, together with a keener perception of one's responsibility.

MARY   You as a class were asked to realize that this channeled teaching is refined until it meets the spiritual needs of the developed soul. Without gladness in one's life, spiritual development comes slowly. Man's goal is to manifest the divine within. Love is the 8th Ray of the Eightfold Path. Love is the whole of religion. From the desert of your heart, let God 's healing waters flow. Bless you, all of you.

LOLA   As we came through a thick forest, we absorbed the energy of the vigorously alive plants and trees. At the edge of the forest, we entered a plateau of enormous width. There in the center was a temple different than any we had seen. Points seemed to extend out toward us. Then from an elevated vantage point, we saw a beautiful star. From its tall slender central tower, waves of color radiated outward and continued to flow beyond our sight. On the top of each of the pointed projections a beautiful fountain rose higher and higher at each musical keynote. We found ourselves attracted to the entrance at the "point" of the star when our keynote sounded. Before it had harmonized with the next note we were inside, following our color along a beautiful corridor which we realized was going inward toward the center.

We were aware of many doors, and as we traveled this corridor, our guidance was to a particular door where our special needs were met. Entering "my" door, I was happy to see Philo, my high guide. As I sat in conference with him, I felt renewed energy being absorbed, and realized this was one of the physical needs I had lately discovered. This energy possessed qualities that affected the mental as well, and a new decision to awaken all faculties to their highest potential was welcomed. I thanked my guide for his loving help through the past and expressed my determination to go on, to listen for his advice and achieve more, knowing he and other teachers and helpers had the power to lift and guide us all when needed.

My expression of gratitude took me to the center where we sat in a circular area elevated from a lower level. Silently enjoying the beauty of a lovely colored fountain rising and falling as musical tones empowered it, we experienced a sense of expectation. Then a voice spoke, and as it did so the fountain rose to the top of the great tower and color radiated out into the universe.

"Your prayers are heard. Live life from your center out. Your desire for the brotherhood of man, right over might, justice, love, peace, you will bring into your world. You are able to carry out that which is revealed to you. Bless you, my children."

MARY Quite a promise in that one, wasn't there?

MARGARET On asking for a memory of something in the Temple of Power, I saw a series of symbols. The first one I interpreted to mean balance, the second one focus, and the third one could have been a door. The next one was a treble clef sign which I knew was clearly a path to power through music.

Then these are several sentences: "Power comes through following the Path, as one is immaculate in heart, mind and soul." "To be Christlike, one must pursue his calling to mastership. Mastership is possible for you who truly yearn and live the life of brotherhood." "Power comes through knowing, seeing, thinking, feeling with the highest mind and adapting the findings to the highest use. Spiritual power is increased in direct ratio to the number of units of effort expended." "To grow in faith is to grow in power."

This temple is specifically designed to show one's individual power plants or implants the ways in which one can be of service both to himself and to others. Power is limitless, infinitely expanding. We concentrate its outpouring through color, song, prayer, the arts, and learn to focus our entire being on an earthly or heavenly objective in service to others. Unceasingly is service rendered here to the highest powers of heaven and earth.

A gradient is gratitude. The rose peach color of gratitude makes the path to the temple easy to climb. I did see the Path as a softly winding golden road. With plenty of gratitude there's plenty of paving and the slope is gentle. With little gratitude there isn't so much paving, there's a steep slope, and it's a dangerous approach to power. God transforms energy through love into light and color, and we are part of that color.

To transform other energies into power, we learn to lift in love and light to our highest consciousness and feel the delicate tints and currents of God's exquisite gifts. Power, rightfully used, is embracing God 's gifts. Power is at all levels of consciousness. Our use of spiritual power is to help focus God's force to assist nature in her best endeavors, heightening the highs, softening the lows.

JEANNE   I stood under a bower, receiving a shower of dry rain the colors of silver and rose. Next, I went down a chasm or sand colored slope toward a body of water. I seemed to go through several power stations or areas where color was poured on me in a process that reminded me of a car wash.

Then I was standing alone in the middle of a large area with the wind blowing. I was surrounded with opaline blue, the 10th color of the Spiritual Arc of Blue, and was aware of help being given me in spiritual balance and in integration of spiritual powers. I next became aware of climbing steep, silver stairs with a group. Above us the whole way were a series of silver white arches. Over the temple were rose and turquoise clouds and a halo of purples, yellows and pale greens. Color rays seemed to pull one into the atmosphere until I found myself in a room where delicate rays of the 12th color of the Spiritual Arc of Green were being beamed in on strong concentrated energy, denoting at-one-ment with God and illumination. More and more light has been added as the soul has sought advancement. Illumination guides the steps as the seeker listens to the inner voice of spirit and follows that guidance.

I noticed that the room had pillars and walls of gold. I went through a door the grass green color of the 4th of the Spiritual Arc of Green, meaning reality of life and acceptance of life's challenges. The yellowish tone of enlightenment in the green adds increased perception. This acceptance short circuits self deception, removes fear and resentment and opens new doors to a greater, clearer reality. The vibration of this ray works in large or small problems, in a life threatening situation or in an irritating daily chore. It can provide enlightened energy. Acceptance of the challenge brings help from higher sources.

I entered a room decorated like a mosque in soft, clear blue tinted emerald greens, the 6th color of the Spiritual Arc of Blue, designating spiritual life present in the physical, a sign of rebirth. This color shows one who is reevaluating his priorities and approach to differing ideas and problems. The blue overtone in the green symbolizes higher spiritual reality merged into the physical energy of the green. Blended, these two hues lift one's consciousness as they are absorbed and applied in daily living.

I was given tests on renouncing, on overcoming doubts, and on fear. After the testing was complete I found myself in a purple room where I joined my group. I was told that the only way to live was to have the truths of the night work emerge in daily living.

JOHN BASINSKI I had a vision that seemed to be like the center Temple at Ankor, a flight of very steep stairs and an entrance; then beyond it I could see a tall dome. I was looking almost straight up to it.

MARY That's good, John. I'm very glad you got that. On the 7th Plane when we were studying the Temple of the Animation of God's Love, we spoke about four towers. Do you remember? I said we would take up the Dome, or the Great Tower, later. For in the midst of the four towers, we enter the Dome and climb stairs to the powerful Tower. Now that temple is the harmonic of this temple, the great tower, the dome that John speaks of. It has a mystical significance which only those who've climbed to the holy mount fully understand.

161

It's very important, because that dome houses all the power that comes for psychic attention to the earth; all of the power that comes to Earth through any sort of work between the two planes is built in the dome. It's expressed out from the tower itself. And that's something I want you to picture in your mind.

Remember, you didn't go there just once. You've been taken back to those temples many times. You've earned the right to go back through some deed you accomplished, something that you had left undone; something you left off doing that was detrimental to your development. So when you do sit down and think about it at meditation time, try to take a temple with you and see if you can't recall.

ESTHER BARNES   Mary, as I was writing town "Temple of Power," I had this symbol that looks like a point of a star.

MARY   Yes. The point of a star, and there was a star expressed here by Lola. It's very good. Thank you, Esther. You know, if we become its true harmonics in our keynote and our color we can give to another, psychically. We'll be able to sense the presence of another when we're in that world over there and know what they're doing. And it's a wonderful thing when you once get into the rapport of it and you can came back with the thought, I know we both were there. And you can prove it.

In this world of Color, we're on this path, the Path Eightfold, augmented with Color. Now we know that the path isn't easy to follow, no matter how lovely it is. We do, at times, some small thing; it seems almost a pebble along the way will throw us. And yet, if we can acknowledge to ourselves or turn quickly and apologize for having said something that's entirely out of order and then look back and say, is this a habit? Is this something on the defensive? Am I unhappy because my expectation hasn't been fulfilled? These are what we have to take as a part of the training of development, particularly when we're following the Eightfold Path.

Man is born with, euphemistically, a certain amount of fire, water, and testing. And so, the only thing that people can do, even if they're without knowledge of the heaven world, is to throw water when the other person is throwing fire, when there's anger, say something pacifying. If we can see we're arousing the demon of jealousy or wrong thinking of another human being, let's change the subject. And I think we're greater for having done it, are we not?

Every soul carries its own light into the darkness. And there's no soul that God didn't give the light to. As I've told you before, I repeat again, I've never seen one person where the light of life wasn't glowing. I've seen many sick people, and up until the end of the life, that still glowed warmly within them. So to me, it's as if the hand of God reaching out will light our way to understanding. And if there's something about us we don't like, remodel ourselves. The remodeling job starts from within. Picture yourself as another individual, for we're twins within, spiritual and physical. And as in the physical we're walking so swiftly along the way of life, we pick up so many habits, imitations, and shams. The reality of yourself comes through when sitting in a community of souls that are reaching out for development. And I as I read your auras, I'm proud of each one of you, and I'm glorified in the fact that you've made development. Thank you.

We're of two worlds because we nightly go to that world and are exercised there, and the power of that world comes back with us. And it's within our power to pass that on in creative energy and love to others. From the desert of your heart let God's healing waters start. Christ lived, and he left a message for us. Most of all, I want you to uncover the treasure where Christ is cradled in your heart. Let's make it grow, and always turn in great thanks, asking for help. Just know that inasmuch as we can express ourselves in love and truth, just so far will we go in expressing ourselves on the Other Side, and bringing this as messages back to the world.

VIOLET The Temple of Power is a great domed structure with a high tower. It's so substantial and vast that one feels protected and secure just to look at it. As one does this he sees and feels a rhythmic pulsation of light drawing him irresistibly toward a door that opens of its own accord and is exactly right for him. We approach this domed structure with many people, yet each enters alone and exactly where the operation of laws are most needed in his life.

Within, he's given a resting place, and here, in complete surrender, he lies on a couch to be charged with as much of the power needed as he's able to assimilate. Refreshed and renewed, he rises and is shown a reflection of himself, a true picture of his present spiritual condition. He realizes that to be effective he must learn to apply and express his powers in the integration of his daily living. He is impressed with the truth that the use and appreciation of such powers alone increase their maturity. The gracious effulgence of this initiation fills his soul with abundant faith, all of which he needs to meet the earth challenges this spiritual attainment generates. I hear the great Voice: "Be aware and operate from the high tower of the soul in humble dependence and gratitude."

PATTI We go to these temples on the power of Color and under the Band of St. John. But sometimes we go to a temple where there are people of other religions. Do others go there on another type of power?

MARY The power that would motivate them would be called universal power. Think of it as order under God. We encounter Muslims dressed in white; we know them by their dress and their postures. And the Hindus are so lifted that they're approaching Nirvana. So what I'm trying to give you is the picture that no one in God's world is chosen. There are those that are greater in number, masses, in fact. The Jewish faith has great masses going to their temples.

DALE COPE Do those from other teachings receive the benefits of prayer and meditation as we do, or do they have other practices?

MARY People of all faiths grow mentally and spiritually as a result of prayer and meditation. Quiet reflection deepens our will to know.

MARY JEAN COPE Would this also apply to one's confidence in life after death?

MARY Confidence in life after death is at first an act of faith. Our awareness of the oneness of the two worlds, the life within and life after death are deepened through using our spiritual exercises and techniques. There are desirable virtues and helpful aids in the so-called "holy habits" of prayer and meditation, but there's no greater communion with God than to walk or stand alone in the quiet of night ready to hear his voice. Sure as you're listening in faith, he will speak to you, as he speaks to every man in a language he understands. This then, becomes the path of the sandaled feet of the man of Galilee. In this temple, again the voice of our Christ speaks these words: "Development of God's love made manifest is to be lived. Through this gift man receives direction for each day through the power of love."

*****

THE TEMPLE OF UNIVERSALITY

PATTI This is from Mary on the Temple of Universality:

The temple is known as the Temple of the Living God. Faith is its cornerstone. Above its lighted portals is written: "Faith is the intuitive conviction of that which both reason and conscience approve." Please accept this truth and know that your spiritual body is an achievement of beautiful harmony that is full of radiance, filled with abounding joy of harboring a living soul.

Our example, Jesus Christ, healed others by the potency of his knowing that he was one with the source of life. Christ knew God's plans in every cell of his being. He proclaimed with every breath that he was God's shining substance on earth. Think of yourself, seeker, as you can really be God's shining substance manifesting this moment in time and space.

Oh mortal wonderfully made, God hath indeed himself portrayed in this thine orb of singing fire. In thee he speaks his own desire, and every nerve and filament proclaims his bright embodiment. Go forth! Shine as shines the sun, for God and heaven and man are one!

Each morning before you enter upon the tasks and purposes of the new day, review the place that faith holds in the economy of God's plan for your life. Mentally open wide the floodgates of your being to the transforming power of universal faith. Mentally make of yourself the receptive magnet that will enable you to absorb the vital essence of your environment and renew every individual cell of your body.

Don't forget prayer and meditation, for prayer from an honest soul will, in time, make the human countenance its own divine altar. Years of color prayer and thoughts, like ceaseless music shut up within, will travel in vibrant rhythm along nerves of expression until the lines of the living instrument are drawn into perfect correspondence and the harmony of visible form matches the unheard harmonies of the soul. Create within your life an alert and wakeful consciousness. Make it the repository of your life with self control the master key, cheerfulness the color scheme, and self unfoldment the ongoing process.

Principles given you as universal law to be used by the soul in personal responsibility is yours as given in this temple. We hope that something we say here tonight will rest within your consciousness and give you a lift. That's our prayer. Bless you.

GLENN   As we travel along the steep between the Temple of Power toward the Temple of Universality, our whole being is filled with a desire and a realization that the process of life be expanded, extending until the whole universe challenges us. We long to be more at one with inner reality and express that reality outwardly into life itself.

LOLA   We spend time at the testing stations before entering this temple. After having passed the tests on the steeps and climbed the mountain of adaptability, we reach the high plateau of limitless vistas. Rising there in the center is the temple. Many seeking souls are traveling from all directions to reach this new point of truth. Colors of the most beautiful shades guide seekers to the distinct area to which they belong, where a great one awaits. Groups proceed, entering the circular lower part of the temple.

GENE   We mount a spiral stairway. At different intervals along the ascent, colors fuse and harmonize until a high central tower is reached. Walls conduct color to the exterior and into the universe. Inside is a large open room with walls of sparkling crystal. As we're seated, gentle bell like notes begin. Soft colors adapt to an opalescent hue, then into a sparkling white so beautiful we feel lifted to a new level of existence more wonderful than any we had yet experienced.

The Voice speaks: "Faith has brought you on the upward path. Love as I have, for all that has been created is the universal language. Its power is limitless, and by its practice all are restored to universal happiness and oneness."

MARY The Temple of Universality, located high on the scale of temples of the 8th Plane, speaks of achievement. We in our limited way grasp only a small portion of the meaning of the term universal. This injects a new aspect into the value and outlook of the universal. Here we realize the expansiveness of the heart of God, here is the real brotherhood of man, here are found those of kindred minds. There's no race distinction here; all are of one blood drawn together with a common purpose to know, to follow and to worship in spirit and in truth. Here are those of other faiths who through poise and patience may have surpassed us in the art of meditation and insight. Of primal concept, this Temple of Universality invites unification and realization.

The Temple is circular in form, dominated by its central tower that beckons to all mankind. Its walls are of crystal, its steps mirrored. Its bridges of color, its fountains of peace, its clerestory windows and its altar draw to its teaching the multitudes that come from near and far. Color, music and rhythm encircle the temple. Harmony sings its celestial song; unity spreads its cloak about each expectant traveler; brotherhood permeates the scene and a benediction of peace surrounds the lives of all seekers. When speaking of a foundation to the Temple of Universality, one doesn't refer to a structure, but to its teaching, its content.

Teachings from the Temple: God and man are one. You are wonderfully made. Your eyes will be opened. When a door closes another will open. We need a concept of who we are. To overcome is our goal. Give of yourself. Thankfulness opens doors.

Throughout the many temples on all planes we're given testings of fire, water and air to test our faith. When we react with fear, do we think to reach out for the invisible hand of faith? Fear is rooted deeply in us, and the tests we face are tests of faith in a higher power. This Temple of Universality shows us that there is a reason for our being put through the tests of everyday life, and that we meet these tests with our will. In this we've grown universal within ourselves. We've taken in more area of consciousness. We're more aware than we used to be. We know today that no man is an island, that no one lives alone. Carry the idea of universality with you wherever you go.

MARGARET Universality is a blessing in disguise, for it reaps the harvest of all your trials, labors and victories of the path. You give of yourself, your heart, soul, mind and body, that all may be permeated with the essence that is made. Emptied, you infill with new life and new vision, opportunities that were obscure before. Never presume to know universality. It knows you, takes what you have if you're willing to share God's gifts, and then redistributes them so that you benefit from all to whom you have given, knowingly or unknowingly.

We were led first to the Fountain of Peace, where we journeyed through showers of enlightenment to a rain of peace, until our very souls were saturated in color. We ascended pale green steps of selfless desire and found ourselves gazing up into a rotunda that seemed like a parachute full of symbolic meanings. There are mirrored steps which reflect one's understanding.

Another time we crossed a bridge, then saw a flag of the future, which consisted of quite a number of perpendicular stripes, alternating red and white with a white emblem, a circle in the middle. This emblem was not sewed on; it was seen by leaving spaces in the weaving of the red stripes, and symbolized all life force flowing from God to man. The white is the Christ light of purity and maturity.

I wanted to see the dome again, but saw instead a huge representation of a cotton blossom perhaps thirty feet across, its petals curving outward, the stem and sepals perfect. We were told this beautiful representation is the blossoming of the earth in response to Christ's call, that earth will be unspeakably beautiful when our eyes are opened. This week I was aware of many tests, some of which were given in symbolic form. I saw Miriam Abplanalp twice, Bernard, Lola, Sheila, and Mary.

JEANNE I gazed across a large field of many plantings of numerous colors and patterns. All along me were wide walks and flowers in different shades. I was especially impressed with the way a certain portion formed the 5th color of the Spiritual Arc of Green. I stood on an end looking north, and nearby saw Miriam Albplanalp holding a bean stalk. Next I was aware of being inside the temple, and of a long, low lavender and pink corridor that led into great blue halls, open and spacious, seeming almost to be made of air and mirrors. I was given a test on tolerance, and shown the colors of sympathetic understanding and spiritual wisdom, as well as new growth and basic understanding.

Given a test of fear, I was aware of a clearance of old habits of thinking based on false conditioning. These patterns were rearranged in the light of reality. In another test, I wanted to step in and take over a situation a friend was mishandling, but realized I didn't have the right interfere in someone else's life. This lesson was so strongly impressed on my mind, so firmly stamped on the subconscious by the teachers, that I believe it will bear fruit in my next earth test involving this. I saw Grace, Helen von Gehr, Margaret, Esther Estabrook, Connie and Sylvia.

I told Sylvia I had just seen a house with an extra unused room in it, and Sylvia said, "I have a house with lots of rooms I never use." I asked her why she didn't use them, and Sylvia replied, "I just haven't gotten around to it yet." I entered an area with a pale blue background with pink flowers. Here I was given greater facility in color, in order to better understand it as an inner language, so words will be less necessary in understanding one's spiritual progress and internal states of the self and others. This was part of training in reading auras, the instruction of how color speaks and conveys its message telepathically, so ones understanding is simultaneous with the message of the color.

I had a very dramatic experience where a woman and I were together; I was standing slightly behind her, as a casual acquaintance. However, I was told by a teacher that this woman had to be my close companion for eternity. I understood then that this woman was an aspect of myself, and when the teachers said I could either make peace with her or go on warring forever, I was flooded with understanding of what this woman represented as well as what eternity meant.

As I saw the implications of what a horror eternity without peace would mean, a flood of emotions welled up, wherein I protested vehemently against this terrible fate and was given the reasons for the existing conditions, which came in a series of images too swift to record; however three of them which impressed me with their emotional force were: a toy duck, a high door in shadows, and a clock. Included in this swift movie screen imagery were strong impressions in the subconscious, deeply buried fears which were revealed to me and unmasked as silly and unfounded.

I was very shaken by these revelations, and the guides placed me in a bed to rest, from where I called Mary's name many times. I felt I had experienced an enormous cleansing and release, that a heavy block had been removed. Afterward, I visited a chapel of pale blue colors, which seemed like part of a cathedral. This whole week I have had the feeling of going deeper into the temples and of climbing further up the Mount of Renunciation.

BARBARA I'd like to say that this was a very wonderful and interesting experience for me, because I'm finding more and more that experiences in the temples go along with experiences I'm having in earth life. The other thing that to me was wonderful is that I didn't know – I hadn't looked to see what the next temple was, and I didn't realize it was Universality until I looked it up after coming back with this recall:

My eyes feasted on an altar cloth made of purest, whitest snow. From a strangely shaped, four rail altar, I ascended, floated up a mighty stairway. There I found myself looking out of a huge open window, before which a great one who seemed to be my Lord Christ was standing. I saw the expanding vastness of the universe with billow upon billow of expanding, undulating colors. As I became aware of these I felt myself borne out upon them. I was one with this expansion, one with the universe itself. As this experience waned, I was once again in a small room where a woman in a radiant pale blue robe awaited to instruct me. This was her message to me, or part of it:

"You can't stop time, for there is no time. You can't contain space, for there is no space. You belong now to no one race, no nation, no clime, for you have been initiated into the eternal, expanding universe of the great Christ."

CARMEN AUSTIN I've been to many temples, but I've never seen Miriam and Mary until last Wednesday. All I remember was I was going through with a lot of people, and there were the helpers who gathered around you two, Mary and Miriam, and I remember that there were people sitting around waiting for the next step.

ESTHER BARNES In meditation I saw the exquisite center of a flower, its stamens the color of the blood of Christ, bursting into tiny, budlike flowers at the end. It was a true temptation to go on to further vision, and then I saw more of this particular flower. It was a bloom of many petals, the color of the yellow of illumination.

MIRIAM WILLIS One approaches the Temple of Universality through an area of color softly enfolding and in a vibration of music. At first was the rose purple amethyst of divine imagination that merged into the royal purple of faith, revealing great depth of love in rich, blue red plum, lifting one over a bridge of sympathetic understanding in brilliant rose fuchsia to the red plum of spiritual wisdom and into the greyed pink lavender of harmony, the blending of all these colors of the Spiritual Arc of Purple, combined into gossamer vapor in lighter tones, softly veiled with silver light.

The music and rhythm are beyond words to describe. The intervals of tones seem so much closer and finer than those of earth instruments. There is nothing on earth like it, for this music is the music of the spheres. This color bath brings one forth clothed in his keynote color and in lifted consciousness. One knows the power of God's color rays have empowered him for further experience.

All now is golden sunlight with a vast open area of brilliance and central glory. One's soul knows this is the Temple of Universality, from where the source, the inception of all elements are revealed: the power of fire and its universal action, its varying forms of heat, light, energy; likewise water, its vaporization and condensation, its life-giving action, its mighty power and cleansing force; air, its content contained in material density released in explosive force, its essential, etheric, life-giving elements, its infiltration into all voids on earth and in heaven, its rarified refinement in spirit, and in its compete cycle to its source.

In awe and wonder, one knows that this is God, that all creation is an expression of his magnificent overflow of love, that man is of his substance and can a possess a portion of his powers through universal love. We know the truth of the existence of a creative intelligence to whom we vaguely give the name of God; the truth that behind all outer seeing, the motivating power of the universe is love; the truth that a great individuality came to earth called by Christians the Christ who embodied that love; the truth that both love and intelligence are affects of what is called the will of God, and finally, that only through the development of man's soul can the divine plan manifest.

JEANNE   Miriam's words brought to mind something that I forgot to mention – fire in my experience this past week where I was in bed calling your name. Later on, in addition to the cleansing, I experienced a surge of new feeling of peace and love. I related it to a universal feeling of fire wherein some of the religions talk about the sacred fire being a force.

MARY   That's right. I would relate the fire tests you've taken to the seven tests you took between the temples, and I would relate one of these to the fire test, another to the water test. We fall, sometimes, through the air in a test of fear, and I'm perfectly sure there are few who don't react with fear. What is our reaction? From it, do we reach out for the hand of faith? It's an invisible hand, an invisible something. Most of these things we believe in we have taken by faith. We started from infancy with a certain amount of faith.

As we become adults, each generation brings something just a little more alerted to the earth. And so, as the old tree shows its age and eventually has to be lopped off, and we've lived the length of life that we can be useful, then a kind Father takes us home, where we can become more useful than we can be here.

Again I feel that in this Temple of Universality this week, we understand there's a reason for us being put through the tests of everyday life, and that as we meet them, we've grown universal within ourselves. We've taken in more area of consciousness. We're more aware than we used to be. We so often draw back and say, "the club dues are getting so high now, there are so many people joining now; I used to enjoy it but I don't anymore."

There's responsibility when you go into a big group of people. You're going to be asked to do something you don't care to do. Personal responsibility was brought up no end of times this past week through our teachers in the temples. We do hate anything that disturbs our balance and equilibrium. In this temple, we've moved into a new era of accepting people as they are without judgment. This is evidence of our growth. This is the test. Your progress is written in the Temple of Universality.

There's a richness, an aliveness and an expanded awareness in this temple when you see every nation coming in to pay tribute to their God. We saw the poise of the Hindu, passive, happy looking people, peaceful people. I especially thought how wise the Hindu was. We could all wish for the poise of the Hindu, the quietness, how he sits serenely for hours at a stretch. We took in four temples, we came back and the Hindus were still there. Afterwards, I got to thinking about it. I thought, my goodness, are they still there? I don't believe that our group of eighty, there wasn't one that didn't turn their head to that particular group of the most passive, poised, happy looking people at peace.

Upon our return, we visited a small temple, the Temple of Remembrance, where we stayed for about an hour that night. I asked, "Do you remember having gone here before?" And no one had ever been there before, they thought.

"Well," I said, "didn't you sit outside the temple last year?" And nearly everyone recalled yes, they did. "Why didn't you go in last year?" I asked. "What have you overcome this year?" Do you know what five people said? "I'm not as critical as I was." So they had moved into a new era of accepting people as they are, not setting themselves up as an example to judge others by, which is such an easy thing to do. I saw great growth by taking you to the

Temple of Universality. The reckoning of your own progress was written right there.

God has cherished you enough that he has built within you a consciousness, a desire to improve yourself, to find something higher than just the levels of consciousness where so many other people live, and to pull yourself up by your bootstraps. It can be done. God has fulfilled a promise. Christ gave it to every one of us. "Follow thou me." And he said, "I will show you many things." Have you not seen many things come to pass?

LENORE One night I seemed to be in a science class, and I saw a blackboard with formulas on it, like chemistry formulas. It was a symbol for something very profound that became embedded in my consciousness.

BARBARA I came back with two vivid dreams. I'll tell about the one Monday night. I'd been singing and playing for a group of people. I remember I was talking with them, and it seemed to be between two phases of a program. We all went together into a great hall. A children's choir was singing. The children were dressed in white robes with red capes about their shoulders. It wasn't like the conventional red-tie thing. They were singing a melodious hymn of praise to God. One little child sang out a solo part in this clear young voice. It was just glorious and numinous.

MIRIAM ALBPLANALP This is the electromagnetic sound-color we aurically answer in response to the song of love from above. It's the prime healing force of all, the therapy of therapies, the eternal blessing of ultimate, omnipotent peace, omni-dimensional and timeless. The instrument in joyous harmony with the music of the spheres, each sounding his keynote, each radiating the concurrent color, each energizing spiritual atomic fission, is man raised to live his heritage. This is man as he is in minute number who can be in infinite magnitude; man raised to Christ Consciousness and living in the promised heaven on earth.

JUNE How would you interpret a water test, what it does for us?

MARY When we're going into the temples, our emotions are reconciled or we don't go inside. A water test is a cleansing. It's breaking of old molds of thinking. There's a clean, new mold starting again. It's a great change. And you come back purified.

In the Temple of Universality we learned more about Jesus Christ than we had learned at previous temples this past year. We learned that the pattern of his life was so simple. The pattern was walking, loving, thinking, giving. He met up with the same things we're living with today. We saw that man alone creates his own difficulties. And so, to be a disciple of that teacher, we have to first see ourselves as the mirror shows us, look into the eyes of the person we are, study the soul values.

No door is closed in our life that another one won't open if we're on the way. I've seen doors closed over and over again and waited until the other one opened. I had the faith to know that door will open. We can live in immortality now, because the worlds are one great world. Don't ever forget that. Try to take that every once in a while in your consciousness, and know that you're not living just for this earth. It's one great world.

You pray "world without end, amen." The Master said it, and we have prayed that prayer.

So what do you say that tonight we go home with the thought that we have on that side of life been privileged to enter that world as seekers. We've been cleansed. Life sometimes seems a desert, hot and dry, no water of life for us. Again, rains fall in our life, we're refreshed, and growth takes place. I believe we must have those arid times in order to appreciate the times when everything is right. So let us know that each life reveals to itself the pattern that was in that soul when God created it. Every man was created by the Architect of the Universe, the pattern of his life given to the soul itself.

MARGARET In this temple we're reminded that one of the greatest reasons, in fact, the single most important reason we're living this life on this earth is to better experience and express love.

****

THE TEMPLE OF TESTING

JEANNE In this temple I experienced tests of two lions, the lions of fear and selfishness – followed by tests on honesty and fairness. I was given glimpses of where I was last year at this time, and the growth I've attained was registered. I was told that I'm now more aware of guidance and the teachers' presence in my life as well as the answers to prayer. It was shown I've improved in gratitude, tolerance, faith, spiritual sight and hearing, as well as understanding. At this point I found myself in an area of the 11th color of the Spiritual Arc of Yellow, with many flowers around. This made me happy, as this color is a ray of developing action, feeding and stimulating spiritual growth.

It was here I heard a voice saying, "I am that I am." I also saw a vision of my guardian angel surrounded with my keynote color and four angelic beings in a silvery white cloud. In this temple I was given further insights into others. In one test, its entirety was given to me as a synopsis ahead of time, and I knew how it would have to be played out. I also recall watching water tests in progress.

I was given further insights into wrong turns on the path, and new facets were revealed I hadn't previously been aware of. Mary and Miriam were in a room to indicate new conditions and higher states of consciousness. This room contained symbols for beautiful spiritual qualities which I was very attracted to and wanted to acquire.

Here I saw that integrating mistakes and carryovers of past lives was necessary to explain certain fears that I have in this life. There was an interplay of symbols which I was able to follow accurately and understand intuitively. Many buried things emerged and I saw certain directions either changed or are in the process of changing. A bell like Pavolov's dog rang simultaneously with directions and conditioning.

I was aware of a spot on my forehead between the eyes where a beam of peach and gold light was being directed, and at the same time the bell rang, words of guidance were impressed on me or a warning given that mistakes of the past not be repeated in the future. I was given tests on judgment involving the character of others and what is of value and importance in several cases where I was the judge.

Traveling this Eightfold Path on the 8th Plane, we've seen how through repetition, one learns. It's been proven that repeated action can change the nervous system physically, altering both synaptic strength and connections.

Many surprises and revelations came. In each instance where I had either made a mistake or was not yet firm in purpose and resolution, the truth was impressed and driven home, and I was able to see things far more clearly than before. Several times I was aware of saying, "I'll certainly know better next time."

PATTI The temple is built on a foundation of solid rock. I saw a white, rectangular temple with colonnades of orchid color. I saw a round pool with mist rising from it in shades of rose. There was much lawn area, as of a grand estate. Roses filled the vision. I saw much lavender, and then a huge silver door of some shining metal with a slightly yellow-gold glistening surface. One seems alone wandering through a stately mansion or castle of stone. One is impelled about by the desire to know of ancient traditions on which people have built. I was in a Hall of Learning that was part of this temple, a place for reestablishment of ties to one another, deeply rooted in ancient patterns and ways. We're brought back to a feeling of wholeness and stability within ourselves, a collecting and centralizing of consciousness as a culmination of effort, and yet an affirmation of stability that will prepare us for the next rung of the ladder in our heavenly ascent through testing. A tremendous fountain showers down.

MARY Very good description.

The Temple of Testing reminds us that we've been exposed to new truths, urged to higher thinking and shown that a change in our nature is paramount. There's been new insight into beauty not heretofore seen. Words of wisdom brought to light have opened new doors of thinking and response. There has been a parting of the veil of the temple where the spirit of the Lord comes shining through to lift us to new heights. We realize we walk not alone; we know there's a plan for our lives, we know that there is an adversary and we know there's a need of a coalition, an alliance and fellowship with the guides and teachers and with each other.

As we grow and our chemistry changes, we find the things we've left undone seem more easily done. We pick up those different events and scan them, and if it's possible to undo a wrong we undo that wrong. Oftentimes I liken it unto a tapestry we're weaving. Some of us weave bright colors into the tapestry of life and others the dull colors, according to mood. And as we get into the heavenly pattern of weaving into our lives, we find those brilliant colors. We find that the soul sends forth an enlightenment of color we never realized was there. Therefore, when we've become enlightened and walk aware of the coloring of that world, it is reflected back here.

All right. Tomorrow's the last day to live, and you're going over to the other world to live; you awaken to the life there and realize you're the same person, that your mind is developed to a certain place, that the elements of your body will be changed, but that you can think.

After you leave Restland, you're taken by teachers to the Halls of Remembrance, where you'll be able to read the plan of your life here on Earth. And as you read the pattern, you'll think you did better than expected, because you've overcome so much. Yet you'll wonder as you look at your record, "Why was I so stupid?" You weren't stupid, you were having an experience that made you a better person.

The Temple of Testing, found high in the 8th Plane on the left side, is there by reason of the All Knowing's provision for the need of time and place to reevaluate our lives, to take inventory of our spiritual attainments, to test our inner fibers relative to our dedication. The signals now become light of illumination, direction of the spirit and loving kindness.

The past year in the study of the Planes of Heaven comes to a close, which reminds us that much has been given to bring this steady flow of teachings from and about the temples and surroundings. Our part in this is to assimilate these findings, then to make use of them in our lives and pass this knowledge on to another that they, too, may be enlightened.

######

ABOUT THE AUTHOR

Jeanne Rejaunier graduated from Vassar College, and did postgraduate studies in Paris, Florence, Rome, and at UCLA. While a student at Vassar, she began a career as a professional model, and subsequently became an actress in Manhattan, Hollywood and Europe, appearing on and off Broadway, in films and television, on magazine covers internationally and as the principal in dozens of network television commercials.

Rejaunier achieved international success with the publication of her first novel, *The Beauty Trap*, which sold over one million copies and became Simon and Schuster's fourth best seller of the year, the film rights to which were purchased outright by Avco-Embassy. Rejaunier has publicized her books in national and international tours on three continents in five languages. Her writing has been extolled in feature stories in *Life*, *Playboy*, *Mademoiselle*, *Seventeen*, *BusinessWeek*, *Fashion Weekly*, *Women's Wear*, *W*, *McCalls*, *American Homemaker*, *Parade*, *Let's Live*, *Marie-Claire*, *Epoca*, *Tempo*, *Sogno*, *Cine-Tipo*, *Stern*, *Hola*, *The New York Times*, *The Los Angeles Times*, *The Washington Post*, and countless other publications.

Rejaunier has written several other books (see "Books by Jeanne Rejaunier").

Branching out as a filmmaker, Rejaunier produced, directed, filmed, and edited the four hour documentary, *The Spirit of '56: Meetings with Remarkable Women*.

******

BOOKS BY JEANNE REJAUNIER

The Beauty Trap
The Motion and the Act
Affair in Rome
Mob Sisters
Odalisque at the Spa
Everybody's Husband
Hollywood Sauna Confidential
My Sundays with Henry Miller
Titans of the Muses (with Noreen Nash)
Planes of the Heavenworld
Everything You Always Wanted to Know About Heaven But Didn't Know Where to Ask
The Kingdom of Heaven and 4th Dimensional Consciousness
The Afterlife in the Here and Now
Living in Eternity Now
Modeling From the Ground Up
The 50 Best Careers in Modeling
Runway to Success
Astrology For Lovers (with Lu Ann Horstman)
Astrology and Your Sex Life (with Maria Graciette)
The Paris Diet (with Noreen Nash and Monique de Warren)
The Complete Idiot's Guide to Food Allergy (with Lee Freund, M.D.)
The Complete Idiot's Guide to Migraines and Other Headaches (with Dennis Fox, M.D.)
Japan's Hidden Face (with Toshio Abe)
The Video Jungle (written under nom de plume)

****

WHAT READERS ARE SAYING ABOUT
THE PLANES OF HEAVEN SERIES

"A new universe of limitless visions and ideas."

"A totally new and exciting slant on spirituality."

"Groundbreaking ... unlike anything I've ever read before."

"What a priceless gift to share with those who are seeking a spiritual uplift!"

"How to prepare for your own transition by visiting the Planes of Heaven in the here and now."

"Discover how other Planes of Consciousness intertwine with our earthly life and vice versa."

"The descriptions and the wisdom imparted are amazing and will go a long way toward readers' understanding of life and the Afterlife. Having the verification of 50 different people is a wonderful assurance not only of what awaits us after we die, but will enrich our lives now as well."

"Ms. Rejaunier has handled this material with rare expertise and dedication."

"An excellent resource to any and all readers inquiring about 'what happens after death', as your energy (Soul) is released back into the Universe (Heaven)."

"This book offers a rare insight into Heaven."

"Any reader interested in spirituality, metaphysics, personal development, and self-help, would be fascinated by this interesting and compellingly written book."

######

Made in the USA
San Bernardino, CA
01 May 2020